W9-DBW-162

CONTENTS.

NOTE

This translation has been revised by Dr. Albert R. Chandler, Assistant Professor of Philosophy in Ohio State University. Changes have been made only for the sake of increased fidelity to the original text. The translation still remains substantially that of Dr. Montgomery. Cross references to the *Correspondence* have been added in footnotes to facilitate ready reference from one letter to another.

GOTTFRIED WILHELM
LEIBNIZ

DISCOURSE ON METAPHYSICS
CORRESPONDENCE WITH ARNAULD
MONADOLOGY

INTRODUCTION BY PAUL JANET

TRANSLATED BY
GEORGE MONTGOMERY

OPEN COURT PUBLISHING COMPANY
LA SALLE, ILLINOIS 61301

Translation copyrighted © in 1902 by Open Court Publishing
Company.

Ninth printing 1988
Tenth printing 1989
Eleventh printing 1990
Twelfth printing 1991
Thirteenth printing 1993

Discourse on Metaphysics

Library of Congress Catalog Card Number: 51-45405
ISBN 0-87548-030-6

INTRODUCTION.

By PAUL JANET.

When Descartes, in the first half of the seventeenth century, said that there are only two kinds of things or substances in nature, namely, extended substances and thinking substances, or bodies and spirits; that, in bodies, everything is reducible to extension with its modifications of form, divisibility, rest and motion, while in the soul everything is reducible to thinking with its various modes of pleasure, pain, affirmation, reasoning, will, etc. . . ; when he in fact reduced all nature to a vast mechanism, outside of which there is nothing but the soul which manifests to itself its existence and its independence through the consciousness of its thinking, he brought about the most important revolution in modern philosophy. To understand its significance however an account must be given of the philosophical standpoint of the time.

In all the schools at that time the dominant theory was that of the Peripatetics, altered by time and misunderstood, the theory of *substantial forms*. It posited in each kind of substance a special *entity* which constituted the reality and the specific difference of that substance independently of the relation of its parts. For example, according to a Peripatetic of the time, "fire differs from water not only through the position of its parts but through an entity which belongs to it quite distinct from the materials. When a body changes its condition, there is no change in the parts, but one form is supplanted by another." * Thus, when water becomes ice, the Peripatetics claimed that a new form substituted itself in place of the preceding form to constitute a new body. Not only did they admit primary or basal entities, or substantial forms to explain the differences in substances, but for small changes also, and for all the sensible qualities they had what were called *accidental forms:* thus hardness, heat, light were beings quite different from the bodies in which they were found.

*L. P. Lagrange, *Les Principes de la Philosophie contre les Nouveaux Philosophes.*—See Bouillier's *Histoire de la Philosophie Cartesienne*, Vol. I, Chap. 26.

To avoid the difficulties inherent in this theory, the School-men were led to adopt infinite divisions among the substantial forms. In this way the Jesuits of Coïmbre admitted three kinds of these forms: first, the being which does not receive its existence from a superior being and is not received into an inferior subject,—this being is God; second, the forces which receive their being from elsewhere without being themselves received into matter,—these are the forms which are entirely free from any corporeal concretion; third, the forms dependent in every respect, which obtain their being from a superior cause and are received into a subject,—these are the accidents and the substantial forms which determine matter.

Other Schoolmen adopted divisions still more minute and distinguished six classes of substantial forms, as follows: first, the forms of primary matter or of the elements; second, those of inferior compounds, like stones; third, those of higher compounds, like drugs; fourth those of living beings, like plants; fifth, those of sensible beings, like animals; sixth, above all the rest, the reasoning (*rationalis*) substantial form which is like the others in so far as it is the form of a body but which does not derive from the body its special function of thinking.

Some have thought, perhaps, that Molière, Nicole, Malebranche and all those who in the seventeenth century ridiculed the substantial forms, calumniated the Peripatetic Schoolmen and gratuitously imputed absurdities to them. But they should read the following explanation, given by Toletus, of the production of fire: "The substantial form of fire," says Toletus, "is an active principle by which fire with heat for an instrument produces fire." Is not this explanation even more absurd than the *virtus dormitiva?* The author goes on to raise an objection, that fire does not always come from fire. To explain this he proceeds, "I reply that there is the greatest difference between the accidental and the substantial forms. The accidental forms have not only a repugnance but a definite repugnance, as between white and black, while between substantial forms there is a certain repugnance but it is not definite, because the substantial form repels equally all things. Therefore it follows that white which is an accidental form results only from white and not from black, while fire can result from all the substantial forms capable of producing it in air, in water or in any other thing."

The theory of substantial or accidental forms did more than to lead to nonsense like the above; it introduced errors which stood in the way of any clear investigation of real causes. For example, since some bodies fell toward the earth while others rose in the air, it was said that gravity was the substantial form of the former and lightness of the latter. Thus heavy and light bodies were distinguished as two classes of bodies having properties essentially different, and they were kept from the inquiry whether these apparently different phenomena did not have an identical cause and could not be explained by the same law. It was thus again that seeing water rise in an empty tube, instead of inquiring under what more general fact this phenomena could be subserved, they imagined a *virtue*, an occult *quality*, a *hatred* on the part of the vacuum, and this not only concealed the ignorance under a word void of sense but it made science impossible because a metaphor was taken for an explanation.

So great had become the abuse of the *substantial forms*, the *occult qualities*, the *sympathetic virtues*, etc., that it was a true deliverance when Gassendi on the one hand and Descartes on the other founded a new physics on the principle that there is nothing in the body which is not contained in the mere conception of bodies, namely extension. According to these new philosophers all the phenomena of bodies are only modifications of extension and should be explained by the properties inherent in extension, namely, form, position, and motion. Upon this principle nothing happens in bodies of which the understanding is not able to form a clear and distinct idea. Modern physics seems to have partially confirmed this theory, when it explains sound and light by movements (vibrations, undulations, oscillations, etc.), either of air or of ether

It has often been said that the march of modern science has been in the opposite direction from the Cartesian philosophy, in that the latter conceives of matter as a dead and inert substance while the former represents it as animated by forces, activities and energies of every kind. This it seems to me is to confuse two wholly different points of view, that is the physical and the metaphysical points of view. The fact seems to be that from the physical point of view, science has rather followed the line of Descartes, reducing the number of occult qualities and as far as possible explaining all the phenomena in terms of motion. In this way all the problems tend to become problems of mechanics; change of position, change of form, change of motion—these are the principles to which our physicists and our chemists have recourse whenever they can.

It is therefore wrong to say that the Cartesian line of thought has completely failed and that modern science has been moving away from it more and more. On the contrary we are witnessing the daily extension of mechanicalism in the science of our time. The question takes on a different phase when it is asked whether mechanicalism is the final word of nature, whether it is self-sufficient, in fact whether the principles of mechanicalism are themselves mechanical. This is a wholly metaphysical question and does not at all affect positive science; for the phenomena will be explained in the same way whether matter is thought of as inert, composed of little particles which are moved and combined by invisible hands, or whether an interior activity and a sort of spontaneity is attributed to them. For the physicist and for the chemist, forces are only words representing unknown causes. For the metaphysician they are real activities. It is metaphysics, therefore, and not physics which is rising above mechanicalism. It is in metaphysics that mechanicalism has found, not its contradiction, but its completion through the doctrine of dynamism. It is this latter direction that philosophy has mainly taken since Descartes and in this the prime mover was Leibniz.*

---

*We give here in a note the résumé of Leibniz's life and the names of his principal works. Leibniz (Gottfried Wilhelm) was born at Leipzig in 1646. He lost his father at the age of six years. From his very infancy he gave evidence of remarkable ability. At fifteen years of age he was admitted to the higher branches of study (philosophy and mathematics) which he pursued first at Leipzig and then at Jena. An intrigue not very well understood prevented his obtaining his doctor's degree at Leipzig and he obtained it from the small university of Altdorf near Nuremberg, where he made the acquaintance of Baron von Boineburg, who became one of his most intimate friends and who took him to Frankfort. Here he was named as a councillor of the supreme court in the electorate of Mainz, and wrote his first two works on jurisprudence, *The Study of Law* and *The Reform of the Corpus Juris.* At Frankfort also were written his first literary and philosophical works and notably his two treatises on motion: *Abstract Motion*, addressed to the Academy of Sciences at Paris, and *Concrete Motion*, addressed to the Royal Society at London. He remained with the Elector till the year 1672, when he began his journeys. He first went to Paris and then to London, where he was made a member of the Royal Society. Returning to Paris he remained till 1677, when he made a trip through Holland, and finally took up his residence at Hanover, where he was appointed director of the library. At Hanover he lived for ten years, leading a very

In order to understand Leibniz's system we must not forget a point to which sufficient attention has not been made, namely, that Leibniz never gave up or rejected the mechanicalism of Decartes. He always affirmed that everything in nature could be explained mechanically; that, in the explanation of phenomena, recourse must never be had to occult causes; so far indeed did he press this position that he refused to admit Newton's attraction of gravitation, suspecting it of being an occult quality: while, however, Leibniz admitted with Descartes the application of mechanicalism he differed from him in regard to the basis of it and he is continually repeating that if everything in nature is mechanical, geometrical and mathematical the source of mechanicalism is in metaphysics.*

Descartes explained everything geometrically and mechani-

---

busy life. He contributed to the founding of the *Acta Eruditorum*, a sort of journal of learning. From 1687 to 1691, at the request of his patron, Duke Ernst-Augustus, he was engaged in searching various archives in Germany and Italy for the writing of the history of the house of Brunswick. To him the Academy of Berlin, of which he was the first president, owes its foundation. The last fifteen years of his life were given up principally to philosophy. In this period must be placed the *New Essays*, the *Theodicy*, the *Monadology*, and also his correspondence with Clarke, which was interrupted by his death—November 14, 1716. For fuller details, see Guhrauer's learned and complete biography, 2 vols, Breslau, 1846. During the life-time of Leibniz, aside from the articles in journals, only some five of his writings were published, including his doctor's thesis, *De Principio Individui* (1663), and the *Théodicée* (1710). After his death (1716) all his papers were deposited in the library at Hanover, where they are to-day, a great part of them (15,000 letters) still unpublished. In 1717-1719 appeared the Correspondence with Locke; in 1720 a German translation of the *Monadology;* in 1765 his *Oeuvres Philosophiques, etc.*, including the *New Essays on the Human understanding;* in 1768 Duten's edition of his works in six volumes; in 1840 appeared Erdmann's edition of his works, including among other unpublished writings the original French of the *Monadology.* The *Correspondence with Arnauld* and the *Treatise on Metaphysics* were first published by Grotefend in 1840. Gerhardt published Leibniz's mathematical works 1843 to 1863, and the *Philosophical Works* (seven volumes), 1875-1890. In 1900 Paul Janet, who had already published the *Philosophical Works* (1866) in two volumes, brought out a second edition, revised and enlarged. The first English translation of Leibniz's works was made by Professor G. M. Duncan, who included in one volume all of the better known shorter works (1890). This was followed in 1896 with a translation of the *New Essays* by A. G. Langley. Latta's translation of some of the shorter works, including the *Monadology*, has earned a well-merited reputation, and Russell's work on Leibniz's philosophy contains much that is suggestive to a translator.

*Letter to Schulemburg (Dutens, T. III, p. 332): "The Cartesians rightly felt that all particular phenomena of bodies are produced mechanically, but they failed to see that the sources of mechanicalism in turn arise in some other cause." Letter to Rémond de Montmort (Erdman, *Opera Philosophica*, p. 702): "When I seek for the ultimate reasons of mechanicalism and the laws of motion I am surprised to discover that they are not to be found in mathematics and that we must turn to metaphysics."—See also: *De Natura Ipsa*, 3; *De Origine Radicali; Animadversiones in Cartesium* Guhrauer, p. 80), etc.

cally, that is by extension, form, and motion, just as Democritus had done before; but he did not go farther, finding in extension the very essence of corporeal substance. Leibniz's genius showed itself when he pointed out that extension does not suffice to explain phenomena and that it has need itself of an explanation. Brought up in the scholastic and peripatetic philosophy, he was naturally predisposed to accord more of reality to the corporeal substance, and his own reflections soon carried him much farther along the same line.

It is also worth noticing, as Guhrauer has said in his *Life of Leibniz*, that it was a theological problem which put Leibniz upon the track of reforming the conception of substance. The question was rife as to the real presence in transubstantiation. This problem seemed inexplicable upon the Cartesian hypothesis, for if the essence of a body is its extension, it is a contradiction that the same body can be found in several places at the same time. Leibniz, writing to Arnauld in 1671, says he thinks he has found the solution to this great problem, since he has discovered "that the essence of a body does not consist in extension, that the corporeal substance, even taken by itself, is not extension and is not subject to the conditions of extension. This would have been evident if the real character of substance had been discovered sooner."

Leaving aside this point, however, the following are the different considerations which led Leibniz to admit non-mechanical principles as above corporeal mechanicalism, and to reduce the idea of the body to the idea of active indivisible substances, entelechies or monads, having innate within themselves the reason for all their determinations.

1. The first and principal reason which Leibniz brings up against Descartes is that, "If all that there is in bodies is extension and the position of the parts, then when two bodies come into contact and move on together after the contact, that one which was in motion will carry along the body at rest without losing any of its velocity, and the difference in the sizes of the bodies will effect no change," which is contrary to experience. A body in motion which comes in contact with one at rest loses some of its velocity and its direction is modified, which would not happen if the body were purely passive. "Higher conceptions must therefore be added to extension, namely, the conceptions of substance, action and force; these

latter carry the idea that that which suffers action, acts reciprocally and that that which acts is reacted upon." *

2. Extension cannot serve to give the reason for the
changes which take place in bodies, for extension with its
various modifications constitutes what is called in the school
terminology extrinsic characteristics, whence nothing can result
for the being itself; whether a body be round or square does
not affect its interior condition, nor can any particular change
result for it.† Furthermore every philosophy which is exclu-
sively mechanical is obliged to deny change and to hold that
everything is changeless and that there are only modifications
of position or displacements in space or motion. Who does
not see, however, that motion itself is a change, and should
have its reason in the being which moves or which is moved,
for even passive motion must correspond to something in the
essence of the body moved? Besides if corporeal elements
differ from one another through form, why have they one form
rather than any other? Epicurus talks to us of round and
hooked atoms. Why is a certain atom round and another
hooked? Should not the reason be in the very substance of the
atom? Therefore form, position, motion and all the extrinsic
modifications of bodies should emanate from an internal
principle analogous to that which Aristotle calls *nature* or
entelechy.‡

3. Extension cannot be substance. On the contrary it presupposes substance. "Aside from extension there must be a
subject which is extended, that is, a substance to which continuity appertains. For extension signifies only a continued
repetition or multiplication of that which is expanded, a plurality, a continuity or co-existence of parts and consequently it
does not suffice to explain the real nature of expanded or repeated
substance whose conception precedes that of repetition." §

4. Another reason given by Leibniz is that the conception of

---

* Letter, Whether the essence of bodies consists in extension, 1691 (Erdmann, Vol. 27, p. 112).

"†Extension is an attribute which cannot constitute a complete being
from it can be obtained neither action nor change; it expresses merely a
present condition but in no case the past or future, as the conception of a
substance should."—Letter to Arnauld.

‡ *Confessio Naturae Contra Artheista*, 1668, Erdm., p. 45. Leibniz in
this little treatise proves: 1st, that bodies and indeed atoms have not in
themselves the reason for their forms; 2d, that they have not the reason for
their motion; 3d, that they have not the reason for their coherence.

§ Extract from a letter (Erdmann, Vol. 28, p. 115): Examination of the
principles of Malebranche (Erdmann, p. 692).

substance necessarily implies the idea of unity. No one thinks
that two stones very far apart form a single substance. If now
we imagine them joined and soldered together, will this juxta-
position change the nature of things? Of course not; there
will always be two stones and not a single one. If now we
imagine them attached by an irresistible force, the impossibility
of separating them will not prevent the mind from distin-
guishing them and will not prevent their remaining two and
not one. In a word every compound is no more a single substance than is a pile of sand or a sack of wheat. We might
as well say that the employees of the India Company formed
a single substance.* It is evident therefore that a compound
is never a substance and in order to find the real substance we
must attain unity or the indivisible. To say that there are no
such unities is to say that matter has no elements, in other
words that it is not made up of substance but it is a pure phenomenon like the rainbow. The conclusion is then either that
matter has no substantial reality or else it must be admitted
that it is reducible to simple and consequently unextended
elements, called *monads*.

5. Leibniz brings forward another argument in behalf of
his theory of monads. This is that the essence of every substance is in force, which fact is as true of the soul as of the body.
It can be proved *a priori*. Is it not evident that a being really
exists only in so far as it acts? A being absolutely passive
would be a pure nothing, and would involve a contradiction;
or, by hypothesis, receiving everything from outside and having nothing through itself, it would have no characteristic, no
attribute and hence would be a pure nothing. The mere fact
of existence, therefore, already supposes a certain force and a
certain energy.

Leibniz presses this thought of the activity of substances so
far that he even admits no degree of passivity. According to

* "If the parts which act together for a common purpose, more properly
compose a substance than do those which are in contact, then all the officials of the India Company would much better constitute a real substance
than would a pile of stones. What else, however, is a common purpose
rather than a resemblance or indeed an orderliness which our minds notice
in different things? If on the other hand the unity by contact be made the
basis, other difficulties arise. The parts of solid bodies are united perhaps
only by the pressure of surrounding bodies, while in themselves and in their
substance there is no more union than in a heap of sand, *arena sine calce*.
Why do many rings when interlaced to form a chain compose a veritable
substance rather than when there are openings so that they can be taken
apart? . . . They are all fictions of the mind." (Letter to Arnauld).

him, no substance is, properly speaking, passive. Passion in
a substance is nothing else than an action considered bound
to another action in another substance. Every substance acts
only through itself and cannot act upon any other. The
monads have no windows through which to receive anything
from outside. They do not undergo any action and consequently are never passive. All that takes place in them is the
spontaneous development of their own essence. All that there
is, is that the states of each one correspond to the states of all
the others. When we consider one of these states in one
monad as corresponding to a certain other state in another
monad, in such a way that the latter is the condition of the
former, the first state is called a *passion* and the second an
action. There is, therefore, between all monad-substances a
pre-established harmony, in accordance with which each one
represents (or *expresses*, as Leibniz says) the whole universe.
But this is ever only the development of its own activity.

In restoring to created substances the activity which the
Cartesian school had too much sacrificed, Leibniz thought to
contribute to the clearer distinction between the created and
the Creator. He justly remarked that the more the activity of
the created things is diminished, the more necessary becomes
the intervention of God, in such a way that if all activity in
created things is suppressed, then we must say that it is God
who brings everything in them to pass and who is at the same
time their being and their action (*operari et esse*). What
difference, however, is there between this point of view and
that of Spinoza? Would we not thus make nature the life and
the development of the divine nature? In fact, by this hypothesis, nature is reduced to a mass of modes of which God is the
substance. He, therefore, is all that there is of reality in bodies
as well as in spirits.

To these five fundamental reasons given by Leibniz it will
perhaps be allowed us to add a few particular considerations.

Those who deny that the essence of bodies is only in
force, either admit the vacuum with the atomists, ancient and
modern, or else like the Cartesians they do not admit it. Let
us take up each of these positions separately.

For the atomists, disciples of Democritus and of Epicurus,
or of Gassendi, the universe is composed of two elements, the
vacuum and the plenum, on the one hand space and on the

other hand bodies. The bodies are reducible to a certain number of solid corpuscles, indivisible, with differing forms, heavy and animated by an essential and spontaneous motion. These are the atoms which by their coming together constitute bodies.

Now it is evident that atoms in taking the place of other atoms, successively occupy in empty space places that are adequate to them, which have exactly the same extension and the same forms as the respective atoms. If at the moment when an atom is motionless in some place we imagine lines drawn following its contours (as when an object is being traced for transferring), is it not clear that if the atom were removed, we should have preserved its effigy, or a sort of silhouette, its geometric form upon a foundation of empty space? We should obtain thus a portion of space, which I will call an empty atom, in contrast with the full atom which was there before.

Now I ask the atomists to explain what distinguishes the full atom from the empty one, what are the characteristics that may be found in one and not in the other. Is it the being extended? No, for the empty atom is extended like the full atom. Is it the having a form? No, for the empty atom has a form as has the full atom and exactly the same form. Is it the being indivisible? No, for it is still more difficult to understand the divisibility of space than of the body. In a word everything which depends on extension is the same in the empty atom as in the full atom. But the empty atom is not a body and contains nothing corporeal; therefore extension is not the essence of bodies and perhaps does not constitute a part of this essence. May we say that it is the motion which distinguishes the full atom from the empty atom? But before beginning to move the atom must have already been something, because that which is nothing in itself can be neither at rest, nor in motion. Motion, therefore, is a dependent and subordinate phenomenon which already presupposes a defined essence. If we examine carefully we will see that what really distinguishes the full atom from the empty atom is its solidity or weight. Neither solidity nor weight, however, are modifications of extension; both come from force. It is accordingly, force and not extension which constitutes the essence of the body.

Turning now to those who, like the Cartesians, are unwill-

ing to admit the possibility of a vacuum and maintain that all
space is full, the demonstration is still more simple, for we may
ask in what filled space, taken in its entirety, differs from
empty space taken in its entirety. Both are infinite; both are
ideally divisible and both are really indivisible; both are susceptible of modalities in form or of geometrically defined forms.
Perhaps it will be claimed that in full space the particles are
movable and can supplant one another; in this case we are
back in the preceding line of argument and we shall ask in
what these movable particles are distinguished from the
immovable particles of space among which they move. Thus
the Cartesians, like the atomists, will be obliged to recognize
that the plenum is distinguished from the vacuum only by
resistance, solidity, motion, activity, in a word, force.

To those who reproach the Leibnizian conception with
idealizing matter too much, it may be replied that matter
taken in itself is necessarily ideal and super-sensible.   Of
course it cannot be said that a body is only an assembly of
subjective modifications.   The Berkeleyan idealism is a super-
ficial idealism, which will not stand examination; for when I
shall have reduced the whole universe to a dream of my mind
and to an expansion of myself the question will still remain
whence comes this my dream and what are the causes which
have produced in me so complicated a hallucination; these
causes are outside of me and they go beyond me on every
side; it would therefore be very inappropriate for me to call them
myself, for the I is strictly that of which I have consciousness.
The Fichtean *Ich*, which by reaction against itself thus produces the *nicht-ich* is only a complicated and artificial circum-
locution for saying in a paradoxical form that there is a not-I.
At most, we can conjecture with the absolute idealism that
the I and the not-I are only two faces of one and the same
being, which involves them both in an infinite activity; but
we thus reach a position very far from the idealism of Berkeley.

To return to the idealism of Leibniz, I think it can be shown
a priori that matter taken in itself is something ideal and
super-sensible, at least to those who admit a divine intelligence.
For it will readily be granted that God does not know matter
by means of the senses; for it is an axiom in metaphysics that
God has no senses and consequently cannot have sensations.
Thus: God can be neither warm nor cold; he cannot smell the

odor of flowers; he cannot hear sounds, he cannot see colors; he cannot feel electrical disturbances, etc. In a word, since he is a pure intelligence he can conceive only the purely intelligible; not that he is ignorant of any of the phenomena of nature, only that he knows them in their intelligible reasons and not through their sensible impressions, by means of which creatures are aware of them. Sensibility supposes a subject with senses, organs and nerves, that is, it is a relation between created things. From God's point of view, therefore, matter is not sensible; it is, as the Germans say, *übersinnlich*. The conclusion is easy to draw, namely, that God, being absolute intelligence, necessarily sees things as they are, and conversely the things in themselves are such as he sees them. Matter is, accordingly, such in itself as God sees it, but he sees it only in its ideal and intelligible essence; whence we see that matter is an intelligible something and not something sensible.

To be sure we may not conclude from this point that the essence of matter does not consist in extension, for it could be maintained that extension is an object of pure intelligence quite as well as force. But without taking up the difficulty of disengaging extension from every sensible element, I wish to establish only one thing, namely that Leibniz cannot be reproached with idealizing matter, since this must be done in every system, at least in those which admit a divine *logos* and a foreordaining reason.

One of the most widely spread objections against the monadological system is the impossibilty of composing an extended whole out of non-extended elements. This is Euler's principal objection in one of his Letters to a German Princess and he considered it absolutely definitive because the necessary consequence of such a system would be to deny the reality of extension and of space, and to launch out thus into all the difficulties of the idealistic labyrinth. I think, however, that Euler's objection is not at all insoluble, and that it is even possible to separate the system of monads from the system of the ideality of space. It can be shown that all the questions relating to space can be adjourned or kept back without compromising the hypothesis of the monads.

For, let us suppose with the atomists, with Clarke and Newton, the reality of space, vacuums, and atoms. It is no more difficult to conceive of monads in space than of atoms; a point of indivisible activity might be at a certain point of space and a collection of the points of activity would constitute the mass which we call a body. Now, even if we grant that these points of activity are separated by space, yet when they were taken together they might produce upon the senses the impression of continuous space. Even in the case of what is called a body, say a marble table, every one knows that there are forces, that is to say, vacuums, between the parts. Since these vacuums, however, escape our sense organs, the body appears to us to be continuous, like the circle described by a moving succession of luminous points. In fact the bodies would be composed, as the Pythagoreans have already said, of two elements; the *intervals* (διαστήματα) and the *monads* (μόναδες); except that the Pythagorean monads were mere geometric points, while for Leibniz they are active points, radiating centers of activity, energies.

Regarding the difficulty of admitting into space forces non-extended and consequently having no relation to space, I grant that it is very serious. It cannot be raised, however, by those who consider the soul as a non-extended force and as an individual substance; for they are obliged to recognize that it is in space although in its essence it has no relation to space; there is, therefore, for them no contradiction in holding that a simple force is in space. If, on the other hand, it be denied that the soul is in space, that it is in the body, and even that it is in a certain part of the body, is it not clear that this would be attributing to the soul a character which is true only of God? To be sure, those who consider the soul as a divine idea, an eternal form temporarily united to an individual, might speak thus. Thus regarded, with the idealists or with Spinoza, the soul is not in space. But if the soul is represented as an individual and created substance, how can it be thought of except as in space and in the body to which it is united? Still more, therefore, in the case of monads will we be obliged to admit that they may be in space and then, as we have seen, the appearance of extension is explained without difficulty.

If, now, instead of admitting the reality of space we hold with Leibniz or with Kant that it is ideal, the system of monads offers no longer any serious difficulty, except from the point of view of those who deny the plurality of individual substances. In any case Euler's objection evidently loses its force.

Another difficulty raised against the monadology is that it effaces the distinction between the soul and the body. This difficulty seems to me like the preceding one to be merely apparent. Because in every hypothesis, the essential distinction between the body and the soul is that the body is a composite, while the soul is simple. In order to prove that the soul is not extended the proof is offered that it is not a composite, while the body on the contrary is. Now in Leibniz's hypothesis also, the body is only a composite, only an aggregation of simple elements. What difference does the nature of the elements make in this case? It is the whole, it is the aggregation which we contrast with the soul; and in Leibniz's hypothesis, quite as well as in that of Descartes, the body as an aggregation is wholly incapable of thought.

Some one will reply: "granting all that, the elements are nevertheless single and indivisible like the soul itself and they are therefore of the same nature as the soul—they are souls themselves." This last consequence is very incorrectly drawn, however.

What is meant by the words: "of the same nature"? Does it mean that the monads which compose the body are feeling, thinking, willing beings? Leibniz never said such a thing. What is the basis for affirming that the particles of my body are thinking substances? Let us look at the semblance they have to the soul. Doubtless they are like it single and indivisible substances. But what difficulty does it introduce to admit that the soul and body have common attributes? The atoms, for instance, have they not in common with the soul, existence, indestructibility, self-identity? And does the argument of the identity of the ego in contrast with the changing nature of organized matter, cease to be valid, because the atom is quite as self-identical as the soul? Indeed the indestructibility of the atom is used as an analogy to establish the indestructibility of the soul. If this common character does not prevent their being distinguished, why should their being distinguished be more difficult when they have in common a character essential to all substance, namely, the attribute of activity?

Furthermore, if the atoms of the substance, which constitutes the universe, are indivisible units, the power of thinking is not inconsistent with their conception. They may be thinking substances, and it cannot be denied that in this system a monad may become, if God wishes it, a thinking soul. If on the one hand it is not impossible, there is no way, on the other hand, of proving that it may be so. Why may there not be several orders of monads which are unable to pass from one class to another? Why may there not be monads having merely mechanical properties; others of a higher order, containing the principle of life, like plant souls; still higher sensitive souls; and finally free and intelligent souls endowed with personality and immortality? Leibniz's system is no more opposed than any other to these orders.

If, however, by a bolder hypothesis, the possibility of a monad's passing from one order to another be admitted, there would still be nothing here degrading to the true dignity of man, for, after all it must be recognized that the human soul in its first state is hardly anything more than a plant-soul which lifts itself by degrees to the condition of a thinking soul. Therefore there will be no contradiction in admitting that every monad contains potentially a thinking soul. Should such a hypothesis be repugnant, I still maintain that the monadological system does not force one to it, since monadism quite as well as the popular atomism can admit a scale of substances essentially distinct from one another.

Another objection which the Leibnizian excites, and one which Arnauld does not fail to raise in one of his letters, is that the system of monads weakens the argument of a first mover, since it implies that matter can be endowed with active force and consequently with spontaneous motion. Leibniz does not meet this objection in a convincing manner and says merely that recourse must be had to God to explain the co-ordination of movements. This, however, avoids the point, for the co-ordination has no relation to the argument of the first mover, only to that of the ordering and of the arrangement which is a wholly different matter. We may, however, remark that Leibniz, in order to establish the reality of the force in corporeal substance, much more frequently uses the fact of resistance to motion, than that of the so-called spontaneous motion. For instance, one of his principal arguments is that a moving body, when it comes in contact with another, loses motion in proportion to the resistance which the other opposes to it, and this is what he calls inertia. It is evident, therefore that if a substance in repose reveals itself by its resistance to motion, the argument of the first mover, far from being weakened is, on the contrary, strengthened.

Besides this, even if a spontaneous disposition to movement, be admitted in the elements of bodies, yet experience compels us to recognize that this disposition passes over into action only upon the excitation of an exterior action because we never see a body put in motion except in the presence of another. The actual indifference to movement and to repose, which at the present time is called, in mechanics, inertia, must always be admitted, whether we posit in the body a virtual disposition to movement or whether, on the contrary, the body be considered as absolutely passive; in either case there must be a cause determining the motion; it is not necessary that this first cause produce everything in the body moved, and that it should be in some sort the total cause of the motion; sufficient is it for it to be the complementary cause as the Schoolmen used to say.

Furthermore inertia must not be confounded with absolute inactivity. Leibniz showed admirably that an absolutely passive substance would be a pure nothing; that a being is active in proportion as it is in existence; in a word, that to be and to act are one and the same thing. From the fact, however, that a substance is essentially active, it does not nec_essarily follow that it is endowed with spontaneous motion, for the latter is only a special mode of activity and is not the only one. For example, resistance, or impenetrability, is a certain kind of activity, but is not motion. They are mistaken, therefore, who think that the theory of active matter does away with a first cause for motion, because even if motion be essential to matter, we will still have to explain why no portion of matter is ever spontaneously in motion.

In short, according to Leibniz, every being is essentially active. That which does not act does not exist; *quid non agit non existit*. Now, whatever acts is force; therefore, everything is force or a compound of forces. The essence of matter is not, as Descartes thought, inert extension, it is action, effort, energy. Furthermore the body is a compound and the compound presupposes a simple. The forces, therefore, which compose the body are simple elements, unextended—incorporeal atoms. Thus the universe is a vast dynamism, a wise system of individual forces, harmoniously related under the direction of a primordial force, whose absolute activity permits the existence outside of itself of the appropriate activities of created things, which it directs without absorbing them. This system, therefore, may be reduced to three principal points: 1, it makes the idea of force predominate over the idea of substance, or rather reduces substance to force; 2, it sees in extension only a mode of appearance of force and compares the bodies of simple and unextended elements as more or less analogous, except in their degree, to what is called the soul; 3, it sees in the forces not only general agents or modes of action of a universal agent, as have the scientists, but it sees also individual principles, both substances and causes which are inseparable from the material, or rather which constitute matter itself; Dynamism thus understood, is only universal spiritualism.

In this introduction I have examined the different difficulties which might be raised against the Leibnizian Monadology from the point of view of the Cartesian spiritualism. They have still to be examined from the point of view of those who deny the plurality of substances, that is, from the Spinozistic or pantheistic point of view. Here, however, come in a wholly different class of ideas, which we cannot enter upon without extending this introduction beyond measure. We will merely say that the force of Leibniz's system is in the fact of individuality, of which the advocates of the unity of substance have never been able to give an explanation. It is true, we must pass here from the objective to the subjective standpoint, because it is in the consciousness that the individuality manifests itself in the most striking manner, while in nature it is more veiled. One's position, therefore, should be taken in the region of the individual consciousness in order to combat Spinozism. This point of view has been particularly developed in our day by Maine de Biran and by his school. We have been content to mention it merely, not desiring to skim over a problem which is connected with the knottiest points of metaphysics and of the philosophy of religion.

METAPHYSICS.

METAPHYSICS.

I. Concerning the divine perfection and that God does everything in the most desirable way.

The conception of God which is the most common and the most full of meaning is expressed well enough in the words: God is an absolutely perfect being. The implications, however, of these words fail to receive sufficient consideration. For instance, there are many different kinds of perfection, all of which God possesses, and each one of them pertains to him in the highest degree.

We must also know what perfection is. One thing which can surely be affirmed about it is that those forms or natures which are not susceptible of it to the highest degree, say the nature of numbers or of figures, do not permit of perfection. This is because the number which is the greatest of all (that is, the sum of all the numbers), and likewise the greatest of all figures, imply contradictions. The greatest knowledge, however, and omnipotence contain no impossibility. Consequently power and knowledge do admit of perfection, and in so far as they pertain to God they have no limits.

Whence it follows that God who possesses supreme and infinite wisdom acts in the most perfect manner not only metaphysically, but also from the moral standpoint. And with respect to ourselves it can be said that the more we are enlightened and informed in regard to the works of God the more will we be disposed to find them excellent and conforming entirely to that which we might desire.

II. Against those who hold that there is in the works of God no goodness, or that the principles of goodness and beauty are arbitrary.

Therefore I am far removed from the opinion of those who maintain that there are no principles of goodness or perfection in the nature of things, or in the ideas which God has about them, and who say that the works of God are good only through the formal reason that God has made them. If this position were true, God, knowing that he is the author of things, would not have to regard them afterwards and find them good, as the Holy Scripture witnesses. Such anthropological expressions are used only to let us know that excellence is recognized in regarding the works themselves, even if we do not consider their evident dependence on their author. This is confirmed by the fact that it is in reflecting upon the works that we are able to discover the one who wrought. They must therefore bear in themselves his character. I confess that the contrary opinion seems to me extremely dangerous and closely approaches that of recent innovators who hold that the beauty of the universe and the goodness which we attribute to the works of God are chimeras of human beings who think of God in human terms. In saying, therefore, that things are not good according to any standard of goodness, but simply by the will of God, it seems to me that one destroys, without realizing it, all the love of God and all his glory; for why praise him for what he has done, if he would be equally praiseworthy in doing the contrary? Where will be his justice and his wisdom if he has only a certain despotic power, if arbitrary will takes the place of reasonableness, and if in accord with the definition of tyrants, justice consists in that which is pleasing to the most powerful? Besides it seems that every act of willing supposes some reason for the willing and this reason, of course, must precede the act. This is why, accordingly, I find so strange those expressions of certain philosophers who say that the eternal truths of metaphysics and Geometry, and consequently the principles of goodness, of justice, and of perfection, are effects only of the will of God. To me it seems that all these follow from his understanding, which does not depend upon his will any more than does his essence.

III. Against those who think that God might have made things better than he has.

No more am I able to approve of the opinion of certain modern writers who boldly maintain that that which God has made is not perfect in the highest degree, and that he might have done better. It seems to me that the consequences of such an opinion are wholly inconsistent with the glory of God. *Uti minus malum habet rationem boni, ita minus bonum habet rationem mali.* I think that one acts imperfectly if he acts with less perfection than he is capable of. To show that an architect could have done better is to find fault with his work. Furthermore this opinion is contrary to the

Holy Scriptures when they assure us of the goodness of God's work. For if comparative perfection were sufficient, then in whatever way God had accomplished his work, since there is an infinitude of possible imperfections, it would always have been good in comparison with the less perfect; but a thing is little praiseworthy when it can be praised only in this way.

I believe that a great many passages from the divine writings and from the holy fathers will be found favoring my position, while hardly any will be found in favor of that of these modern thinkers. Their opinion is, in my judgment, unknown to the writers of antiquity and is a deduction based upon the too slight acquaintaince which we have with the general harmony of the universe and with the hidden reasons for God's conduct. In our ignorance, therefore, we are tempted to decide audaciously that many things might have been done better.

These modern thinkers insist upon certain hardly tenable subtleties, for they imagine that nothing is so perfect that there might not have been something more perfect. This is an error. They think, indeed, that they are thus safeguarding the liberty of God. As if it were not the highest liberty to act in perfection according to the sovereign reason. For to think that God acts in anything without having any reason for his willing, even if we overlook the fact that such action seems impossible, is an opinion which conforms little to God's glory. For example, let us suppose that God chooses between A and B, and that he takes A without any reason for preferring it to B. I say that this action on the

part of God is at least not praiseworthy, for all
praise ought to be founded upon reason which *ex
hypothesi* is not present here.   My opinion is that
God does nothing for which he does not deserve to
be glorified

IV. That love for God demands on our part complete satisfaction with and acquiescence in that which he has done.

The general knowledge of this great truth that
God acts always in the most perfect and most
desirable manner possible, is in my opinion the basis
of the love which we owe to God in all things; for
he who loves seeks his satisfaction in the felicity
or perfection of the object loved and in the perfection of his actions. *Idem velle et idem nolle vera
amicitia est.* I believe that it is difficult to love
God truly when one, having the power to change
his disposition, is not disposed to wish for that
which God desires. In fact those who are not
satisfied with what God does seem to me like dissatisfied subjects whose attitude is not very different from that of rebels.   I hold therefore, that on
these principles, to act conformably to the love of
God it is not sufficient to force oneself to be patient,
we must be really satisfied with all that comes to
us according to his will.   I mean this acquiescence
in regard to the past; for as regards the future one
should not be a quietist with the arms folded,
open to ridicule, awaiting that which God will do;
according to the sophism which the ancients called
λόγον ἄεργον, the lazy reason.   It is necessary to act
conformably to the presumptive will of God as
far as we are able to judge of it, trying with all our

might to contribute to the general welfare and particularly to the ornamentation and the perfection of that which touches us, or of that which is nigh and so to speak at our hand. For if the future shall perhaps show that God has not wished our good intention to have its way, it does not follow that he has not wished us to act as we have; on the contrary, since he is the best of all masters, he ever demands only the right intentions, and it is for him to know the hour and the proper place to let good designs succeed.

V. In what the principles of the divine perfection consist, and that the simplicity of the means counterbalances the richness of the effects.

It is sufficient therefore to have this confidence in God, that he has done everything for the best and that nothing will be able to injure those who love him. To know in particular, however, the reasons which have moved him to choose this order of the universe, to permit sin, to dispense his salutary grace in a certain manner,—this passes the capacity of a finite mind, above all when such a mind has not come into the joy of the vision of God. Yet it is possible to make some general remarks touching the course of providence in the government of things. One is able to say, therefore, that he who acts perfectly is like an excellent Geometer who knows how to find the best construction for a problem; like a good architect who utilizes his location and the funds destined for the building in the most advantageous manner, leaving nothing which shocks or which does not display that beauty of which it is capable; like a good householder who employs his property in such a way that there shall be nothing uncultivated or sterile; like a clever machinist who makes his production in the least difficult way possible; and like an intelligent author who encloses the most of reality in the least possible compass.

Of all beings those which are the most perfect and occupy the least possible space, that is to say those which interfere with one another the least, are the spirits whose perfections are the virtues. That is why we may not doubt that the felicity of the spirits is the principal aim of God and that he puts this purpose into execution, as far as the general harmony will permit. We will recur to this subject again.

When the simplicity of God's way is spoken of, reference is specially made to the means which he employs, and on the other hand when the variety, richness and abundance are referred to, the ends or effects are had in mind. Thus one ought to be proportioned to the other, just as the cost of a building should balance the beauty and grandeur which is expected. It is true that nothing costs God anything, just as there is no cost for a philosopher who makes hypotheses in constructing his imaginary world, because God has only to make decrees in order that a real world come into being; but in matters of wisdom the decrees or hypotheses meet the expenditure in proportion as they are more independent of one another. The reason wishes to avoid multiplicity in hypotheses or principles very much as the simplest system is preferred in Astronomy.

VI. That God does nothing which is not orderly, and that it is not even possible to conceive of events which are not regular.

The activities or the acts of will of God are commonly divided into ordinary and extraordinary. But it is well to bear in mind that God does nothing out of order. Therefore, that which passes for extraordinary is so only with regard to a particular order established among the created things, for as regards the universal order, everything conforms to it. This is so true that not only does nothing occur in this world which is absolutely irregular, but it is even impossible to conceive of such an occurrence. Because, let us suppose for example that some one jots down a quantity of points upon a sheet of paper helter skelter, as do those who exercise the ridiculous art of Geomancy; now I say that it is possible to find a geometrical line whose concept shall be uniform and constant, that is, in accordance with a certain formula, and which line at the same time shall pass through all of those points, and in the same order in which the hand jotted them down; also if a continuous line be traced, which is now straight, now circular, and now of any other description, it is possible to find a mental equivalent, a formula or an equation common to all the points of this line by virtue of which formula the changes in the direction of the line must occur. There is no instance of a face whose contour does not form part of a geometric line and which can not be traced entire by a certain mathematical motion. But when the formula is very complex, that which conforms to it passes for irregular. Thus we may say that in whatever manner God might have created the world, it would always have been regular and in a certain order. God, however, has chosen the most perfect, that is to say the one which is at the same time the simplest in hypotheses and the richest in phenomena, as might be the case with a geometric line, whose construction was easy, but whose properties and effects were extremely remarkable and of great significance. I use these comparisons to picture a certain imperfect resemblance to the divine wisdom, and to point out that which may at least raise our minds to conceive in some sort what cannot otherwise be expressed. I do not pretend at all to explain thus the great mystery upon which depends the whole universe.

VII. That miracles conform to the regular order although they go against the subordinate regulations; concerning that which God desires or permits and concerning general and particular intentions.

Now since nothing is done which is not orderly, we may say that miracles are quite within the order of natural operations. We use the term natural of these operations because they conform to certain subordinate regulations which we call the nature of things. For it can be said that this nature is only a custom of God's which he can change on the occasion of a stronger reason than that which moved him to use these regulations. As regards general and particular intentions, according to the way in which we understand the matter, it may be said on the one hand that everything is in accordance with his most general intention, or that which best conforms to the most perfect order he has chosen; on the other hand, however, it is also possible to say that he has particular intentions which are exceptions to the subordinate regulations above mentioned. Of God's laws, however, the most universal, i. e., that which rules the whole course of the universe, is without exceptions.

It is possible to say that God desires everything which is an object of his particular intention. When we consider the objects of his general intentions, however, such as are the modes of activities of created things and especially of the reasoning creatures with whom God wishes to co-operate, we must make a distinction; for if the action is good in itself, we may say that God wishes it and at times commands it, even though it does not take place; but if it is bad in itself and becomes good only by accident through the course of events and especially after chastisement and satisfaction have corrected its malignity and rewarded the ill with interest in such a way that more perfection results in the whole train of circumstances than would have come if that ill had not occurred,—if all this takes place we must say that God permits the evil, and not that he desired it, although he has co-operated by means of the laws of nature which he has established. He knows how to produce the greatest good from them.

VIII. In order to distinguish between the activities of God and the activities of created things we must explain the conception of an individual substance.

It is quite difficult to distinguish God's actions from those of his creatures. Some think that God does everything; others imagine that he only conserves the force that he has given to created things. How far can we say either of these opinions is right?

In the first place since activity and passivity pertain properly to individual substances (*actiones sunt suppositorum*) it will be necessary to explain what such a substance is. It is indeed true that when several predicates are attributes of a single subject and this subject is not an attribute of another, we speak of it as an individual substance, but this is not enough, and such an explanation is merely nominal. We must therefore inquire what it is to be an attribute in reality of a certain subject. Now it is evident that every true predication has some basis in the nature of things, and even when a proposition is not identical, that is, when the predicate is not expressly contained in the subject, it is still necessary that it be virtually contained in it, and this is what the philosophers call *in-esse*, saying thereby that the predicate is in the subject. Thus the content of the subject must always include that of the predicate in such a way that if one understands perfectly the concept of the subject, he will know that the predicate appertains to it also. This being so, we are able to say that this is the nature of an individual substance or of a complete being, namely, to afford a conception so complete that the concept shall be sufficient for the understanding of it and for the deduction of all the predicates of which the substance is or may become the subject. Thus the quality of king, which belonged to Alexander the Great, an abstraction from the subject, is not sufficiently determined to constitute an individual, and does not contain the other qualities of the same subject, nor everything which the idea of this

prince includes. God, however, seeing the individual concept, or hæcceity, of Alexander, sees
there at the same time the basis and the reason of
all the predicates which can be truly uttered regarding him; for instance that he will conquer Darius
and Porus, even to the point of knowing *a priori*
(and not by experience) whether he died a natural
death or by poison,—facts which we can learn only
through history. When we carefully consider the
connection of things we see also the possibility of
saying that there was always in the soul of Alexander marks of all that had happened to him and
evidences of all that would happen to him and
traces even of everything which occurs in the universe, although God alone could recognize them all.

**IX. That every individual substance expresses the
whole universe in its own manner and that in its full
concept is included all its experiences together with all
the attendent circumstances and the whole sequence of
exterior events.**

There follow from these considerations several
noticeable paradoxes; among others that it is not
true that two substances may be exactly alike and
differ only numerically, *solo numero*, and that what St.
Thomas says on this point regarding angels and
intelligences (*quod ibi omne individuum sit species
infima*) is true of all substances, provided that the
specific difference is understood as Geometers
understand it in the case of figures; again that
a substance will be able to commence only through
creation and perish only through annihilation; that
a substance cannot be divided into two nor can one
be made out of two, and that thus the number of

substances neither augments nor diminishes through natural means, although they are frequently transformed. Furthermore every substance is like an entire world and like a mirror of God, or indeed of the whole world which it portrays, each one in its own fashion; almost as the same city is variously represented according to the various situations of him who is regarding it. Thus the universe is multiplied in some sort as many times as there are substances, and the glory of God is multiplied in the same way by as many wholly different representations of his works. It can indeed be said that every substance bears in some sort the character of God's infinite wisdom and omnipotence, and imitates him as much as it is able to; for it expresses, although confusedly, all that happens in the universe, past, present and future, deriving thus a certain resemblance to an infinite perception or power of knowing. And since all other substances express this particular substance and accommodate themselves to it, we can say that it exerts its power upon all the others in imitation of the omnipotence of the creator.

X. That the belief in substantial forms has a certain basis in fact, but that these forms effect no changes in the phenomena and must not be employed for the explanation of particular events.

It seems that the ancients, able men, who were accustomed to profound meditations and taught theology and philosophy for several centuries and some of whom recommend themselves to us on account of their piety, had some knowledge of that which we have just said and this is why they introduced and

maintained the substantial forms so much decried
to-day. But they were not so far from the truth
nor so open to ridicule as the common run of our
new philosophers imagine. I grant that the consideration of these forms is of no service in the
details of physics and ought not to be employed in
the explanation of particular phenomena. In regard
to this last point, the schoolmen were at fault, as
were also the physicians of times past who followed
their example, thinking they had given the reason
for the properties of a body in mentioning the forms
and qualities without going to the trouble of exam-
ining the manner of operation; as if one should be
content to say that a clock had a certain amount
of clockness derived from its form, and should not
inquire in what that clockness consisted. This is
indeed enough for the man who buys it, provided
he surrenders the care of it to someone else. The
fact, however, that there was this misunderstanding
and misuse of the substantial forms should not bring
us to throw away something whose recognition is
so necessary in metaphysics. Since without these
we will not be able, I hold, to know the ultimate
principles nor to lift our minds to the knowledge
of the incorporeal natures and of the marvels of
God. Yet as the geometer does not need to
encumber his mind with the famous puzzle of the
composition of the continuum, and as no moralist,
and still less a jurist or a statesman has need to
trouble himself with the great difficulties which
arise in conciliating free will with the providential
activity of God, (since the geometer is able to make
all his demonstrations and the statesman can complete all his deliberations without entering into

these discussions which are so necessary and important in Philosophy and Theology), so in the same way the physicist can explain his experiments, now using simpler experiments already made, now employing geometrical and mechanical demonstrations without any need of the general considerations which belong to another sphere, and if he employs the co-operation of God, or perhaps of some soul or animating force, or something else of a similar nature, he goes out of his path quite as much as that man who, when facing an important practical question would wish to enter into profound argumentations regarding the nature of destiny and of our liberty; a fault which men quite frequently commit without realizing it when they cumber their minds with considerations regarding fate, and thus they are even sometimes turned from a good resolution or from some necessary provision.

XI. That the opinions of the theologians and of the so-called scholastic philosophers are not to be wholly despised.

I know that I am advancing a great paradox in pretending to resuscitate in some sort the ancient philosophy, and to recall *postliminio* the substantial forms almost banished from our modern thought. But perhaps I will not be condemned lightly when it is known that I have long meditated over the modern philosophy and that I have devoted much time to experiments in physics and to the demonstrations of geometry and that I, too, for a long time was persuaded of the baselessness of those "beings" which, however, I was finally obliged to take up again in spite of myself and as though by force.

The many investigations which I carried on compelled me to recognize that our moderns do not do sufficient justice to Saint Thomas and to the other great men of that period and that there is in the theories of the scholastic philosophers and theologians far more solidity than is imagined, provided that these theories are employed *à propos* and in their place. I am persuaded that if some careful and meditative mind were to take the trouble to clarify and direct their thoughts in the manner of analytic geometers, he would find a great treasure of very important truths, wholly demonstrable.

XII. That the conception of the extension of a body is in a way imaginary and does not constitute the substance of the body.

But to resume the thread of our discussion, I believe that he who will meditate upon the nature of substance, as I have explained it above, will find that the whole nature of bodies is not exhausted in their extension, that is to say, in their size, figure and motion, but that we must recognize something which corresponds to soul, something which is commonly called substantial form, although these forms effect no change in the phenomena, any more than do the souls of beasts, that is if they have souls. It is even possible to demonstrate that the ideas of size, figure and motion are not so distinctive as is imagined, and that they stand for something imaginary relative to our preceptions as do, although to a greater extent, the ideas of color, heat, and the other similar qualities in regard to which we may doubt whether they are actually to be found in the nature of the things outside of us. This is why these latter qualities are unable to constitute "substance" and if there is no other principle of identity in bodies than that which has just been referred to a body would not subsist more than for a moment.

The souls and the substance-forms of other bodies are entirely different from intelligent souls which alone know their actions, and not only do not perish through natural means but indeed always retain the knowledge of what they are; a fact which makes them alone open to chastisement or recompense, and makes them citizens of the republic of the universe whose monarch is God.   Hence it follows that all the other creatures should serve them, a point which we shall discuss more amply later.

XIII. As the individual concept of each person includes once for all everything which can ever happen to him, in it can be seen, *a priori* the evidences or the reasons for the reality of each event, and why one happened sooner than the other.   But these events, however certain, are nevertheless contingent, being based on the free choice of God and of his creatures.   It is true that their choices always have their reasons, but they incline to the choices under no compulsion of necessity.

But before going further it is necessary to meet a difficulty which may arise regarding the principles which we have set forth in the preceding.   We have said that the concept of an individual substance includes once for all everything which can ever happen to it and that in considering this concept one will be able to see everything which can truly be said concerning the individual, just as we are able to see in the nature of a circle all the properties which can be derived from it. But does it not seem that in this way the difference between contingent and necessary truths will be destroyed, that there will be no place for human liberty, and that an absolute fatality will rule as well over all our actions as over all the rest of the events of the world? To this I reply that a distinction must be made between that which is certain and that which is necessary. Every one grants that future contingencies are assured since God foresees them, but we do not say just because of that that they are necessary. But it will be objected, that if any conclusion can be deduced infallibly from some definition or concept, it is necessary; and now since we have maintained that everything which is to happen to anyone is already virtually included in his nature or concept, as all the properties are contained in the definition of a circle, therefore, the difficulty still remains. In order to meet the objection completely, I say that the connection or sequence is of two kinds; the one, absolutely necessary, whose contrary implies contradiction, occurs in the eternal verities like the truths of geometry; the other is necessary only *ex hypothesi*, and so to speak by accident, and in itself it is contingent since the contrary is not implied. This latter sequence is not founded upon ideas wholly pure and upon the pure understanding of God, but upon his free decrees and upon the processes of the universe. Let us give an example. Since Julius Caesar will become perpetual Dictator and master of the Republic and will overthrow the liberty of Rome, this action is contained in his concept, for we have supposed that it is the nature of such a perfect concept of a subject to involve everything, in fact so that the predicate may be included in the subject *ut possit inesse subjecto*. We may say that it is not in virtue of this concept or idea that he is obliged to perform this action, since it pertains to him only because God knows everything. But it will be insisted in reply that his nature or form responds to this concept, and since God imposes upon him this personality, he is compelled henceforth to live up to it. I could reply by instancing the similar case of the future contingencies which as yet have no reality save in the understanding and will of God, and which, because God has given them in advance this form, must needs correspond to it. But I prefer to overcome a difficulty rather than to excuse it by instancing other difficulties, and what I am about to say will serve to clear up the one as well as the other. It is here that must be applied the distinction in the kind of relation, and I say that that which happens conformably to these decrees is assured, but that it is not therefore necessary, and if anyone did the contrary, he would do nothing impossible in itself, although it is impossible *ex hypothesi* that that other happen. For if anyone were capable of carrying out a complete demonstration by virtue of which he could prove this connection of the subject, which is Caesar, with the predicate, which is his successful enterprise, he would bring us to see in fact that the future dictatorship of Caesar had its basis in his concept or nature, so that one would see there a reason why he resolved to cross the Rubicon rather than to stop, and why he gained instead of losing the day at Pharsalus, and that it was reasonable and by consequence assured that this would occur, but one would not prove that it was necessary in itself, nor that the contrary implied a contradiction, almost in the same way in which it is reasonable and assured that God will always do what is best although that which is less perfect is not thereby implied. For it would be found that this demonstration of this predicate as belonging to Caesar is not as absolute as are those of numbers or of geometry, but that this predicate supposes a sequence of things which God has shown by his free will. This sequence is based on the first free decree of God which was to do always that which is the most perfect and upon the decree which God made following the first one, regarding human nature, which is that men should always do, although freely, that which appears to be the best. Now every truth which is founded upon this kind of decree is contingent, although certain, for the decrees of God do not change the possibilities of things and, as I have already said, although God assuredly chooses the best, this does not prevent that which is less perfect from being possible in itelf. Although it will never happen, it is not its impossibility but its imperfection which causes him to reject it. Now nothing is necessitated whose opposite is possible. One will then be in a position to satisfy these kinds of difficulties, however great they may appear (and in fact they have not been less vexing to all other thinkers who have ever treated this matter), provided that he considers well that all contingent propositions have reasons why they are thus, rather than otherwise, or indeed (what is the same thing) that they have proof *a priori* of their truth, which render them certain and show that the connection of the subject and predicate in these propositions has its basis in the nature of the one and of the other, but he must further remember that such contingent propositions have not the demonstrations of necessity, since their reasons are founded only on the principle of contingency or of the existence of things, that is to say, upon that which is, or which appears to be the best among several things equally possible. Necessary truths, on the other hand, are founded upon the principle of contradiction, and upon the possibility or impossibility of the essences themselves, without regard here to the free will of God or of creatures.

XIV. God produces different substances according to the different views which he has of the world, and by the intervention of God, the appropriate nature of each substance brings it about that what happens to one corresponds to what happens to all the others, without, however, their acting upon one another directly.

After having seen, to a certain extent, in what the nature of substances consists, we must try to explain the dependence they have upon one another and their actions and passions. Now it is first of all very evident that created substances depend upon God who preserves them and can produce them continually by a kind of emanation just as we produce our thoughts, for when God turns, so to say, on all sides and in all fashions, the general system of phenomena which he finds it good to produce for the sake of manifesting his glory, and when he regards all the aspects of the world in all possible manners, since there is no relation which escapes his omniscience, the result of each view of the universe as seen from a different position is a substance which expresses the universe conformably to this view, provided God sees fit to render his thought effective and to produce the substance, and since God's vision is always true, our perceptions are always true and that which deceives us are our judgments, which are of us. Now we have said before, and it follows from what we have just said that each substance is a world by itself, independent of everything else excepting God; therefore, all our phenomena that is all things which are ever able to happen to us, are only consequences of our being. Now as the phenomena maintain a certain order conformably to our nature, or so to speak to the world which is in us (from whence it follows that we can, for the regulation of our conduct, make useful observations which are justified by the outcome of the future phenomena) and as we are thus able often to judge the future by the past without deceiving ourselves, we have sufficient grounds for saying that these phenomena are true and we will not be put to the task of inquiring whether they are outside of us, and whether others perceive them also.

Nevertheless it is most true that the perceptions and expressions of all substances intercorrespond, so that each one following independently certain reasons or laws which he has noticed meets others which are doing the same, as when several have agreed to meet together in a certain place on a set day, they are able to carry out the plan if they wish. Now although all express the same phenomena, this does not bring it about that their expressions

are exactly alike. It is sufficient if they are proportional. As when several spectators think they
see the same thing and are agreed about it, although
each one sees or speaks according to the measure
of his vision. It is God alone, (from whom all
individuals emanate continually, and who sees the
universe not only as they see it, but besides in a
very different way from them) who is the cause of
this correspondence in their phenomena and who
brings it about that that which is particular to one,
is also common to all, otherwise there would be no
relation. In a way, then, we might properly say,
although it seems strange, that a particular substance never acts upon another particular substance
nor is it acted upon by it. That which happens to
each one is only the consequence of its complete
idea or concept, since this idea already includes all
the predicates and expresses the whole universe.
In fact nothing can happen to us except thoughts
and perceptions, and all our thoughts and perceptions are but the consequence, contingent it is true,
of our precedent thoughts and perceptions, in such
a way that were I able to consider directly all that
happens or appears to me at the present time, I
should be able to see all that will happen to me or
that will ever appear to me. This future will not
fail me, and will surely appear to me even if all
that which is outside of me were destroyed, save
only that God and myself were left.

Since, however, we ordinarily attribute to other
things an action upon us which brings us to perceive things in a certain manner, it is necessary to
consider the basis of this judgment and to inquire
what there is of truth in it.

XV. The action of one finite substance upon another consists only in the increase in the degrees of the expression of the first combined with a decrease in that of the second, in so far as God has in advance fashioned them so that they shall act in accord.

Without entering into a long discussion it is sufficient for reconciling the language of metaphysics with that of practical life to remark that we preferably attribute to ourselves, and with reason, the phenomena which we express the most perfectly, and that we attribute to other substances those phenomena which each one expresses the best. Thus a substance, which is of an infinite extension in so far as it expresses all, becomes limited in proportion to its more or less perfect manner of expression. It is thus then that we may conceive of substances as interfering with and limiting one another, and hence we are able to say that in this sense they act upon one another, and that they, so to speak, accommodate themselves to one another. For it can happen that a single change which augments the expression of the one may diminish that of the other. Now the virtue of a particular substance is to express well the glory of God, and the better it expresses it, the less is it limited. Everything when it expresses its virtue or power, that is to say, when it acts, changes to better, and expands just in so far as it acts. When therefore a change occurs by which several substances are affected (in fact every change affects them all) I think we may say that those substances, which by this change pass immediately to a greater degree of perfection, or to a more perfect expression, exert power and act, while those which pass to a lesser degree disclose their weakness and suffer. I also hold that every activity of a substances which has perception implies some pleasure, and every passion some pain, except that it may very well happen that a present advantage will be eventually destroyed by a greater evil, whence it comes that one may sin in acting or exerting his power and in finding pleasure.

XVI. The extraordinary intervention of God is not excluded in that which our particular essences express, because their expression includes everything. Such intervention, however, goes beyond the power of our natural being or of our distinct expression, because these are finite, and follow certain subordinate regulations.

There remains for us at present only to explain how it is possible that God has influence at times upon men or upon other substances by an extraordinary or miraculous intervention, since it seems that nothing is able to happen which is extraordinary or supernatural in as much as all the events which occur to the other substances are only the consequences of their natures. We must recall what was said above in regard to the miracles in the universe. These always conform to the universal law of the general order, although they may contravene the subordinate regulations, and since every person or substance is like a little world which expresses the great world, we can say that this extraordinary action of God upon this substance is nevertheless miraculous, although it is comprised in the general order of the universe in so far as it

is expressed by the individual essence or concept
of this substance. This is why, if we understand
in our natures all that they express, nothing is supernatural in them, because they reach out to everything, an effect always expressing its cause, and
God being the veritable cause of the substances.
But as that which our natures express the most perfectly pertains to them in a particular manner, that
being their special power, and since they are limited,
as I have just explained, many things there are
which surpass the powers of our natures and even
of all limited natures   As a consequence, to speak
more clearly, I say that the miracles and the extraordinary interventions of God have this peculiarity
that they cannot be foreseen by any created mind
however enlightened. This is because the distinct
comprehension of the fundamental order surpasses
them all, while on the other hand, that which is
called natural depends upon less fundamental regulations which the creatures are able to understand.
In order then that my words may be as irreprehen-
sible as the meaning I am trying to convey, it will
be well to associate certain words with certain sig-
nifications. We may call that which includes everything that we express and which expresses our
union with God himself, nothing going beyond it,
our essence. But that which is limited in us may be
designated as our nature or our power and in accordance with this terminology that which goes
beyond the natures of all created substances is
supernatural.

XVII. An example of a subordinate regulation in the law of nature which demonstrates that God always preserves the same amount of force but not the same quantity of motion:—against the Cartesians and many others.

I have frequently spoken of subordinate regulations, or of the laws of nature, and it seems that it will be well to give an example. Our new philosophers are unanimous in employing that famous law that God always preserves the same amount of motion in the universe. In fact it is a very plausible law, and in times past I held it for indubitable. But since then I have learned in what its fault consists. Monsieur Descartes and many other clever mathematicians have thought that the quantity of motion, that is to say the velocity multiplied by the mass* of the moving body, is exactly equivalent to the moving force, or to speak in mathematical terms that the force varies as the velocity multiplied by the mass. Now it is reasonable that the same force is always preserved in the universe. So also, looking to phenomena, it will be readily seen that a mechanical perpetual motion is impossible, because the force in such a machine, being always diminished a little by fric-

---

*This term is employed here for the sake of clearness. Leibniz did not possess the concept "mass," which was enunciated by Newton in the same year in which the present treatise was written, 1686. Leibniz uses the terms "body," "magnitude of body," etc. The technical expression "mass" occurs once only in the writings of Leibniz (in a treatise published in 1695), and was there doubtless borrowed from Newton. For the history of the controversy concerning the Cartesian and Leibnizian measure of force, see Mach's *Science of Mechanics*, Chicago, 1893, pp. 272 et seq.—*Trans.*

tion and so ultimately destined to be entirely spent, would necessarily have to recoup its losses, and consequently would keep on increasing of itself without any new impulsion from without; and we see furthermore that the force of a body is diminished only in proportion as it gives up force, either to a contiguous body or to its own parts, in so far as they have a separate movement. The mathematicians to whom I have referred think that what can be said of force can be said of the quantity of motion. In order, however, to show the difference I make two suppositions: in the first place, that a body falling from a certain height acquires a force enabling it to remount to the same height, provided that its direction is turned that way, or provided that there are no hindrances. For instance, a pendulum will rise exactly to the height from which it has fallen, provided the resistance of the air and of certain other

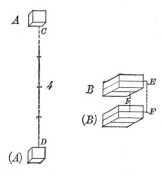

small particles do not diminish a little its acquired force.

I suppose in the second place that it will take as much force to lift a body A weighing one pound to the height CD, four feet, as to raise a body B weighing four pounds to the height EF, one foot. These two suppositions are granted by our new philosophers. It is therefore manifest that the body A falling from the height CD acquires exactly as much force as the body B falling from the height EF, for the body B at F, having by the first supposition sufficient force to return to E, has therefore the force to carry a body of four pounds to the distance of one foot, EF. And likewise the body A at D, having the force to return to C, has also the force required to carry a body weighing one pound, its own weight, back to C, a distance of four feet. Now by the second supposition the force of these two bodies is equal. Let us now see if the quantity of motion is the same in each case. It is here that we will be surprised to find a very great difference, for it has been proved by Galileo that the velocity acquired by the fall CD is double the velocity acquired by the fall EF, although the height is four times as great. Multiplying, therefore, the body A, whose mass is 1, by its velocity, which is 2, the product or the quantity of movement will be 2, and on the other hand, if we multiply the body B, whose mass is 4, by its velocity, which is 1, the product or quantity of motion will be 4. Hence the quantity of the motion of the body A at the point D is half the quantity of motion of the body B at the point F, yet their forces are equal, and there is therefore a great difference between the quantity of motion and the force. This is what we set out to show. We can see therefore how the force ought to be estimated by the quantity of the effect which it is able to produce, for example by the height to which a body of certain weight can be raised. This is a very different thing from the velocity which can be imparted to it, and in order to impart to it double the velocity we must have double the force. Nothing is simpler than this proof and Monsieur Descartes has fallen into error here, only because he trusted too much to his thoughts even when they had not been ripened by reflection. But it astonishes me that his disciples have not noticed this error, and I am afraid that they are beginning to imitate little by little certain Peripatetics whom they ridicule, and that they are accustoming themselves to consult rather the books of their master, than reason or nature.

XVIII. The distinction between force and the quantity of motion is, among other reasons, important as showing that we must have recourse to metaphysical considerations in addition to discussions of extension if we wish to explain the phenomena of matter.

This consideration of the force, distinguished from the quantity of motion is of importance, not only in physics and mechanics for finding the real laws of nature and the principles of motion, and even for correcting many practical errors which have crept into the writings of certain able mathematicians, but also in metaphysics it is of importance for the better understanding of principles. Because motion, if we regard only its exact and formal meaning, that is, change of place, is not something entirely real, and when several bodies change their places reciprocally, it is not possible to determine by considering the bodies alone to which among them movement or repose is to be attributed, as I could demonstrate geometrically, if I wished to stop for it now. But the force, or the proximate cause of these changes is something more real, and there are sufficient grounds for attributing it to one body rather than to another, and it is only through this latter investigation that we can determine to which one the movement must appertain. Now this force is something different from size, from form or from motion, and it can be seen from this consideration that the whole meaning of a body is not exhausted in its extension together with its modifications as our moderns persuade themselves. We are therefore obliged to restore certain beings or forms which they have banished. It appears more and more clear that although all the particular phenomena of nature can be explained mathematically or mechanically by those who understand them, yet nevertheless, the general principles of corporeal nature and even of mechanics are metaphysical rather than geometric, and belong rather to certain indivisible forms or natures as the causes of the appearances, than to the corporeal mass or to extension. This reflection is able to reconcile the mechanical philosophy of the moderns with the circumspection of those intelligent and well-meaning persons who, with a certain justice, fear that we are becoming too far removed from immaterial beings and that we are thus prejudicing piety.

XIX. The utility of final causes in Physics.

As I do not wish to judge people in ill part I bring no accusation against our new philosophers who pretend to banish final causes from physics, but I am nevertheless obliged to avow that the consequences of such a banishment appear to me dangerous, especially when joined to that position which I refuted at the beginning of this treatise. That position seemed to go the length of discarding final causes entirely as though God proposed no end and no good in his activity, or as if good were not to be the object of his will. I hold on the contrary that it is just in this that the principle of all existences and of the laws of nature must be sought, hence God always proposes the best and most perfect. I am quite willing to grant that we are liable to err when we wish to determine the purposes or councils of God, but this is the case only when we try to limit them to some particular design, thinking that he has had in view only a single thing, while in fact he regards everything at once. As for instance, if we think that God has made the world only for us, it is a great blunder, although it may be quite true that he has made it entirely for us, and that there is nothing in the universe which does not touch us and which does not accommodate itself to the regard which he has for us according to the principle laid down above. Therefore when we see some good effect or some perfection which happens or which follows from the works of God we are able to say assuredly that God has purposed it, for he does nothing by chance, and is not like us who sometimes fail to do well. Therefore, far from being able to fall into error in this respect as do the extreme statesmen who postulate too much foresight in the designs of Princes, or as do commentators who seek for too much erudition in their authors, it will be impossible to attribute too much reflection to God's infinite wisdom, and there is no matter in which error is less to be feared provided we confine ourselves to affirmations and provided we avoid negative statements which limit the designs of God. All those who see the admirable structure of animals find themselves led to recognize the wisdom of the author of things and I advise those who have any sentiment of piety and indeed of true philosophy to hold aloof from the expressions of certain pretentious minds who instead of saying that eyes were made for seeing, say that we see because we find ourselves having eyes. When one seriously holds such opinions which hand everything over to material necessity or to a kind of chance (although either alternative ought to appear ridiculous to those who understand what we have explained above) it is difficult to recognize an intelligent author of nature. The effect should correspond to its cause and indeed it is best known through the recognition of its cause, so that it is reasonable to introduce a sovereign intelligence ordering things, and in place of making use of the wisdom of this sovereign being, to employ only the properties of matter to explain phenomena. As if in order to account for the capture of an important place by a prince, the historian should say it was because the particles of powder in the cannon having been touched by a spark of fire expanded with a rapidity capable of pushing a hard solid body against the walls of the place, while the little particles which composed the brass of the cannon were so well interlaced that they did not separate under this impact,—as if he should account for it in this way instead of making us see how the foresight of the conqueror brought him to choose the time and the proper means and how his ability surmounted all obstacles.

XX. A noteworthy disquisition in Plato's Phaedo against the philosophers who were too materialistic.

This reminds me of a fine disquisition by Socrates in Plato's Phaedo, which agrees perfectly with my opinion on this subject and seems to have been uttered expressly for our too materialistic philosophers. This agreement has led me to a desire to translate it although it is a little long. Perhaps this example will give some of us an incentive to share in many of the other beautiful and well balanced thoughts which are found in the writings of this famous author.*

XXI. If the mechanical laws depended upon Geometry alone without metaphysical influences, the phenomena would be very different from what they are.

Now since the wisdom of God has always been recognized in the detail of the mechanical structures of certain particular bodies, it should also be shown in the general economy of the world and in the constitution of the laws of nature. This is so true that even in the laws of motion in general, the plans of this wisdom have been noticed. For if bodies were only extended masses, and motion were only a change of place, and if everything ought to be and could be deduced by geometric necessity from these two definitions alone, it would follow, as I have shown elsewhere, that the smallest body on contact with a very large one at rest would impart to it its own velocity, yet without losing any of the velocity that it had. A quantity of other rules wholly contrary to the formation of a system would also have to be admitted. But the decree of the divine wisdom in preserving always the same force and the same total direction has provided for a

---

* There is a gap here in the MS., intended for the passage from Plato, the translation of which Leibniz did not supply.— *Trans.*

system. I find indeed that many of the effects of
nature can be accounted for in a twofold way, that
is to say by a consideration of efficient causes, and
again independently by a consideration of final
causes. An example of the latter is God's decree
to always carry out his plan by the easiest and most
determined way. I have shown this elsewhere in
accounting for the catoptric and dioptric laws, and
I will speak more at length about it in what follows.

**XXII. Reconciliation of the two methods of explana-
tion, the one using final causes, and the other efficient
causes, thus satisfying both those who explain nature
mechanically and those who have recourse to incorporeal natures.**

It is worth while to make the preceding remark
in order to reconcile those who hope to explain
mechanically the formation of the first tissue of an
animal and all the interrelation of the parts, with
those who account for the same structure by refer-
ring to final causes. Both explanations are good;
both are useful not only for the admiring of the
work of a great artificer, but also for the discovery of
useful facts in physics and medicine. And writers
who take these diverse routes should not speak ill
of each other. For I see that those who attempt to
explain beauty by the divine anatomy ridicule those
who imagine that the apparently fortuitous flow of
certain liquids has been able to produce such a
beautiful variety and that they regard them as over-
bold and irreverent. These others on the contrary
treat the former as simple and superstitious, and
compare them to those ancients who regarded the
physicists as impious when they maintained that

not Jupiter thundered but some material which is
found in the clouds. The best plan would be to
join the two ways of thinking. To use a practical
comparison, we recognize and praise the ability of
a workman not only when we show what designs he
had in making the parts of his machine, but also
when we explain the instruments which he employed
in making each part, above all if these instruments
are simple and ingeniously contrived. God is also
a workman able enough to produce a machine still
a thousand times more ingenious than is our body,
by employing only certain quite simple liquids purposely composed in such a way that ordinary laws
of nature alone are required to develop them so as
to produce such a marvellous effect. But it is also
true that this development would not take place if
God were not the author of nature. Yet I find that
the method of efficient causes, which goes much
deeper and is in a measure more immediate and *a
priori*, is also more difficult when we come to details,
and I think that our philosophers are still very
frequently far removed from making the most of
this method. The method of final causes, however,
is easier and can be frequently employed to find out
important and useful truths which we should have
to seek for a long time, if we were confined to that
'other more physical method of which anatomy is
able to furnish many examples. It seems to me
that Snellius, who was the first discoverer of the laws
of refraction would have waited a long time before
finding them if he had wished to seek out first how
light was formed. But he apparently followed that
method which the ancients employed for Catoptrics,
that is, the method of final causes. Because, while

seeking for the easiest way in which to conduct a
ray of light from one given point to another given
point by reflection from a given plane (supposing
that that was the design of nature) they discovered
the equality of the angles of incidence and reflection, as can be seen from a little treatise by Helio-
dorus of Larissa and also elsewhere. This principle
Mons. Snellius, I believe, and afterwards independently of him, M. Fermat, applied most ingeniously
to refraction. For since the rays while in the same
media always maintain the same proportion of sines,
which in turn corresponds to the resistance of the
media, it appears that they follow the easiest way,
or at least that way which is the most determinate
for passing from a given point in one medium to a
given point in another medium. That demonstration of this same theorem which M. Descartes has
given, using efficient causes, is much less satisfactory. At least we have grounds to think that he
would never have found the principle by that means
if he had not learned in Holland of the discovery
of Snellius.

**XXIII. Returning to immaterial substances we ex-
plain how God acts upon the understanding of spirits
and ask whether one always keeps the idea of what he
thinks about.**

I have thought it well to insist a little upon final
causes, upon incorporeal natures and upon an
intelligent cause with respect to bodies so as to
show the use of these conceptions in physics and in
mathematics. This for two reasons, first to purge
from mechanical philosophy the impiety that is
imputed to it, second, to elevate to nobler lines of

thought the thinking of our philosophers who incline to materialistic considerations alone. Now, however, it will be well to return from corporeal substances to the consideration of immaterial natures and particularly of spirits, and to speak of the methods which God uses to enlighten them and to act upon them. Although we must not forget that there are here at the same time certain laws of nature in regard to which I can speak more amply elsewhere. It will be enough for now to touch upon ideas and to inquire if we see everything in God and how God is our light. First of all it will be in place to remark that the wrong use of ideas occasions many errors. For when one reasons in regard to anything, he imagines that he has an idea of it and this is the foundation upon which certain philosophers, ancient and modern, have constructed a demonstration of God that is extremely imperfect. It must be, they say, that I have an idea of God, or of a perfect being, since I think of him and we cannot think without having ideas; now the idea of this being includes all perfections and since existence is one of these perfections, it follows that he exists. But I reply, inasmuch as we often think of impossible chimeras, for example of the highest degree of swiftness, of the greatest number, of the meeting of the conchoid with its base or determinant, such reasoning is not sufficient. It is therefore in this sense that we can say that there are true and false ideas according as the thing which is in question is possible or not. And it is when he is assured of the possibility of a thing, that one can boast of having an idea of it. Therefore, the aforesaid argument proves that God exists, if he is possible. This is in fact an excellent privilege of the divine nature, to have need only of a possibility or an essence in order to actually exist, and it is just this which is called *ens a se*.

XXIV. What clear and obscure, distinct and confused, adequate and inadequate, intuitive and assumed knowledge is, and the definition of nominal, real, causal and essential.

In order to understand better the nature of ideas it is necessary to touch somewhat upon the various kinds of knowledge. When I am able to recognize a thing among others, without being able to say in what its differences or characteristics consist, the knowledge is confused. Sometimes indeed we may know clearly, that is without being in the slightest doubt, that a poem or a picture is well or badly done because there is in it an "I know not what" which satisfies or shocks us. Such knowledge is not yet distinct. It is when I am able to explain the peculiarities which a thing has, that the knowledge is called distinct. Such is the knowledge of an assayer who discerns the true gold from the false by means of certain proofs or marks which make up the definition of gold. But distinct knowledge has degrees, because ordinarily the conceptions which enter into the definitions will themselves have need of definition, and are only known confusedly. When at length everything which enters into a definition or into distinct knowledge is known distinctly, even back to the primitive conception, I call that knowledge adequate. When my mind understands at once and distinctly all the primitive ingredients of a conception, then we have intuitive knowledge. This is extremely rare as most human knowledge is only confused or indeed assumed. It is well also to distinguish nominal from real definition. I call a definition nominal when there is doubt whether an exact conception of it is possible; as for instance, when I say that an endless screw is a line in three dimensional space whose parts are congruent or fall one upon another. Now although this is one of the reciprocal properties of an endless screw, he who did not know from elsewhere what an endless screw was could doubt if such a line were possible, because the other lines whose ends are congruent (there are only two: the circumference of a circle and the straight line) are plane figures, that is to say they can be described *in plano*. This instance enables us to see that any reciprocal property can serve as a nominal definition, but when the property brings us to see the possibility of a thing it makes the definition real, and as long as one has only a nominal definition he cannot be sure of the consequences which he draws, because if it conceals a contradiction or an impossibility he would be able to draw the opposite conclusions. That is why truths do not depend upon names and are not arbitrary, as some of our new philosophers think. There is also a considerable difference among real definitions, for when the possibility proves itself only by experience, as in the definition of quicksilver, whose possibility we know because such a body, which is both an extremely heavy fluid and quite volatile, actually exists, the definition is merely real and nothing more. If, however, the proof of the possibility is *a priori*, the definition is not only real but also causal as for instance when it contains the possible generation of a thing. Finally when the definition, without assuming anything which requires a proof *a priori* of its possibility, carries the analysis clear to the primitive conception, the definition is perfect or essential.

XXV. In what cases knowledge is added to mere contemplation of the idea.

Now it is manifest that we have no idea of a conception when it is impossible. And in case the knowledge, where we have the idea of it, is only assumed, we do not visualize it because such a conception is known only in like manner as conceptions internally impossible. And if it be in fact possible, it is not by this kind of knowledge that we learn its possibility. For instance, when I am thinking of a thousand or of a chiliagon, I frequently do it without contemplating the idea. Even if I say a thousand is ten times a hundred, I frequently do not trouble to think what ten and a hundred are, because I assume that I know, and I do not consider it necessary to stop just at present to conceive of them. Therefore it may well happen, as it in fact does happen often enough, that I am mistaken in regard to a conception which I assume that I understand, although it is an impossible truth or at least is incompatible with others with which I join it, and whether I am mistaken or not, this way of assuming our knowledge remains the same. It is, then, only when our knowledge is clear in regard to confused conceptions, and when it is intuitive in regard to those which are distinct, that we see its entire idea.

XXVI. Ideas are all stored up within us. Plato's doctrine of reminiscence.

In order to see clearly what an idea is, we must guard ourselves against a misunderstanding. Many regard the idea as the form or the differentiation of our thinking, and according to this opinion we have the idea in our mind, in so far as we are thinking of it, and each separate time that we think of it anew we have another idea although similar to the preceding one. Some, however, take the idea as the immediate object of thought, or as a permanent form which remains even when we are no longer contemplating it. As a matter of fact our soul has the power of representing to itself any form or nature whenever the occasion comes for thinking about it, and I think that this activity of our soul is, so far as it expresses some nature, form or essence, properly the idea of the thing. This is in us, and is always in us, whether we are thinking of it or no. (Our soul expresses God and the universe and all essences as well as all existences.) This position is in accord with my principles that naturally nothing enters into our minds from outside.

It is a bad habit we have of thinking as though our minds receive certain messengers, as it were, or as if they had doors or windows. We have in our minds all those forms for all periods of time because the mind at every moment expresses all its future thoughts and already thinks confusedly of all that of which it will ever think distinctly. Nothing can be taught us of which we have not already in our minds the idea. This idea is as it were the material out of which the thought will form itself. This is what Plato has excellently brought out in his doctrine of reminiscence, a doctrine which contains a great deal of truth, provided that it is properly understood and purged of the error of pre-existence, and provided that one does not conceive of the soul as having already known and thought at some other time what it learns and thinks now. Plato has also confirmed his position by a beautiful experiment. He introduces a small boy, whom he leads by short steps, to extremely difficult truths of geometry bearing on incommensurables, all this without teaching the boy anything, merely drawing out replies by a well arranged series of questions. This shows that the soul virtually knows those things, and needs only to be reminded (animadverted) to recognize the truths. Consequently it possesses at least the idea upon which those truths depend. We may say even that it already possesses those truths, if we consider them as the relations of the ideas.

XXVII. In what respect our souls can be compared to blank tablets and how conceptions are derived from the senses.

Aristotle preferred to compare our souls to blank tablets prepared for writing, and he maintained that nothing is in the understanding which does not come through the senses. This position is in accord with the popular conceptions as Aristotle's positions usually are. Plato thinks more profoundly. Such tenets or practicologies are nevertheless allowable in ordinary use somewhat in the same way as those who accept the Copernican theory still continue to speak of the rising and setting of the sun. I find indeed that these usages can

be given a real meaning containing no error, quite
in the same way as I have already pointed out that
we may truly say particular substances act upon one
another.   In this same sense we may say that
knowledge is received from without through the
medium of the senses because certain exterior things
contain or express more particularly the causes
which determine us to certain thoughts. Because
in the ordinary uses of life we attribute to the soul
only that which belongs to it most manifestly and
particularly, and there is no advantage in going
further.   When, however, we are dealing with the
exactness of metaphysical truths, it is important to
recognize the powers and independence of the soul
which extend infinitely further than is commonly
supposed.   In order, therefore, to avoid misunder-
standings it would be well to choose separate terms
for the two.   These expressions which are in the
soul whether one is conceiving of them or not may
be called ideas, while those which one conceives of
or constructs may be called conceptions, *conceptus*.
But whatever terms are used, it is always false to
say that all our conceptions come from the so-called
external senses, because those conceptions which
I have of myself and of my thoughts, and consequently of being, of substance, of action, of
identity, and of many others came from an inner
experience.

XXVIII. The only immediate object of our percep-tions which exists outside of us is God, and in him alone is our light.

In the strictly metaphysical sense no external
cause acts upon us excepting God alone, and he is

in immediate relation with us only by virtue of our continual dependence upon him. Whence it follows that there is absolutely no other external object which comes into contact with our souls and directly excites perceptions in us. We have in our souls ideas of everything, only because of the continual action of God upon us, that is to say, because every effect expresses its cause and therefore the essences of our souls are certain expressions, imitations or images of the divine essence, divine thought and divine will, including all the ideas which are there contained. We may say, therefore, that God is for us the only immediate external object, and that we see things through him. For example, when we see the sun or the stars, it is God who gives to us and preserves in us the ideas and whenever our senses are affected according to his own laws in a certain manner, it is he, who by his continual concurrence, determines our thinking. God is the sun and the light of souls, *lumen illuminans omnem hominem venientem in hunc mundum*, although this is not the current conception. I think I have already remarked that during the scholastic period many believed God to be the light of the soul, *intellectus agens animæ rationalis*, following in this the Holy Scriptures and the fathers who were always more Platonic than Aristotelian in their mode of thinking. The Averroists misused this conception, but others, among whom were several mystic theologians, and William of Saint Amour, also I think, understood this conception in a manner which assured the dignity of God and was able to raise the soul to a knowledge of its welfare.

XXIX. Yet we think directly by means of our own ideas and not through God's.

Nevertheless I cannot approve of the position of certain able philosophers who seem to hold that our ideas themselves are in God and not at all in us. I think that in taking this position they have neither sufficiently considered the nature of substance, which we have just explained, nor the entire extension and independence of the soul which includes all that happens to it, and expresses God, and with him all possible and actual beings in the same way that an effect expresses its cause. It is indeed inconceivable that the soul should think using the ideas of something else. The soul when it thinks of anything must be affected effectively in a certain manner, and it must needs have in itself in advance not only the passive capacity of being thus affected, a capacity already wholly determined, but it must have besides an active power by virtue of which it has always had in its nature the marks of the future production of this thought, and the disposition to produce it at its proper time. All of this shows that the soul already includes the idea which is comprised in any particular thought.

XXX. How God inclines our souls without necessitating them; that there are no grounds for complaint; that we must not ask why Judas sinned because this free act is contained in his concept, the only question being why Judas the sinner is admitted to existence, preferably to other possible persons; concerning the original imperfection or limitation before the fall and concerning the different degrees of grace.

Regarding the action of God upon the human

will there are many quite different considerations which it would take too long to investigate here. Nevertheless the following is what can be said in general. God in co-operating with ordinary actions only follows the laws which he has established, that is to say, he continually preserves and produces our being so that the ideas come to us spontaneously or with freedom in that order which the concept of our individual substance carries with itself. In this concept they can be foreseen for all eternity. Furthermore, by virtue of the decree which God has made that the will shall always seek the apparent good in certain particular respects (in regard to which this apparent good always has in it something of reality expressing or imitating God's will), he, without at all necessitating our choice, determines it by that which appears most desirable. For absolutely speaking, our will as contrasted with necessity, is in a state of indifference, being able to act otherwise, or wholly to suspend its action, either alternative being and remaining possible. It therefore devolves upon the soul to be on guard against appearances, by means of a firm will, to reflect and to refuse to act or decide in certain circumstances, except after mature deliberation. It is, however, true and has been assured from all eternity that certain souls will not employ their power upon certain occasions.

But who could do more than God has done, and can such a soul complain of anything except itself? All these complaints after the deed are unjust, inasmuch as they would have been unjust before the deed. Would this soul a little before committing the sin have had the right to complain of God as

though he had determined the sin.   Since the determinations of God in these matters cannot be foreseen, how would the soul know that it was pre-
ordained to sin unless it had already committed the
sin?   It is merely a question of wishing to or not
wishing to, and God could not have set an easier or
juster condition.   Therefore all judges without
asking the reasons which have disposed a man to
have an evil will, consider only how far this will is
wrong.   But, you object, perhaps it is ordained
from all eternity that I will sin.   Find your own
answer.   Perhaps it has not been.   Now then,
without asking for what you are unable to know and
in regard to which you can have no light, act according to your duty and your knowledge.   But, some
one will object; whence comes it then that this
man will assuredly do this sin?   The reply is easy.
It is that otherwise he would not be a man.   For
God foresees from all time that there will be a
certain Judas, and in the concept or idea of him
which God has, is contained this future free act.
The only question, therefore, which remains is why
this certain Judas, the betrayer who is possible only
because of the idea of God, actually exists.   To
this question, however, we can expect no answer
here on earth excepting to say in general that it is
because God has found it good that he should exist
notwithstanding that sin which he foresaw.   This
evil will be more than overbalanced.   God will
derive a greater good from it, and it will finally
turn out that this series of events in which is
included the existence of this sinner, is the most
perfect among all the possible series of events.   An
explanation in every case of the admirable econ-

omy of this choice cannot be given while we are sojourners on earth. It is enough to know the excellence without understanding it. It is here that must be recognized *altitudinem divitiarum*, the unfathomable depth of the divine wisdom, without hesitating at a detail which involves an infinite number of considerations. It is clear, however, that God is not the cause of ill. For not only after the loss of innocence by men, has original sin possessed the soul, but even before that there was an original limitation or imperfection in the very nature of all creatures, which rendered them open to sin and able to fall. There is, therefore, no more difficulty in the supralapsarian view than there is in the other views of sin. To this also, it seems to me can be reduced the opinion of Saint Augustine and of other authors: that the root of evil is in the negativity, that is to say, in the lack or limitation of creatures which God graciously remedies by whatever degree of perfection it pleases him to give. This grace of God, whether ordinary or extraordinary has its degrees and its measures. It is always efficacious in itself to produce a certain proportionate effect and furthermore it is always sufficient not only to keep one from sin but even to effect his salvation, provided that the man co-operates with that which is in him. It has not always, however, sufficient power to overcome the inclination, for, if it did, it would no longer be limited in any way, and this superiority to limitations is reserved to that unique grace which is absolutely efficacious. This grace is always victorious whether through its own self or through the congruity of circumstances.

**XXXI. Concerning the motives of election; concern-
ing faith foreseen and the absolute decree and that
it all reduces to the question why God has chosen and
resolved to admit to existence just such a possible person, whose concept includes just such a sequence of free
acts and of free gifts of grace. This at once puts an end
to all difficulties.**

Finally, the grace of God is wholly unprejudiced
and creatures have no claim upon it. Just as it is
not sufficient in accounting for God's choice in his
dispensations of grace to refer to his absolute or
conditional prevision of men's future actions, so it
is also wrong to imagine his decrees as absolute
with no reasonable motive. As concerns foreseen
faith and good works, it is very true that God has
elected none but those whose faith and charity he
foresees, *quos se fide donaturum praescivit.* The
same question, however, arises again as to why God
gives to some rather than to others the grace of
faith or of good works. As concerns God's ability
to foresee not only the faith and good deeds, but
also their material and predisposition, or that which
a man on his part contributes to them (since there
are as truly diversities on the part of men as on
the part of grace, and a man although he needs to
be aroused to good and needs to become converted,
yet acts in accordance with his temperament),—as
regards his ability to foresee there are many who
say that God, knowing what a particular man will
do without grace, that is without his extraordinary
assistance, or knowing at least what will be the
human contribution, resolves to give grace to those
whose natural dispositions are the best, or at any rate
are the least imperfect and evil. But if this were the

case then the natural dispositions in so far as they were good would be like gifts of grace, since God would have given advantages to some over others; and therefore, since he would well know that the natural advantages which he had given would serve as motives for his grace or for his extraordinary assistance, would not everything be reduced to his mercy? I think, therefore, that since we do not know how much and in what way God regards natural dispositions in the dispensations of his grace, it would be safest and most exact to say, in accordance with our principles and as I have already remarked, that there must needs be among possible beings the person Peter or John whose concept or idea contains all that particular sequence of ordinary and extraordinary manifestations of grace together with the rest of the accompanying events and circumstances, and that it has pleased God to choose him among an infinite number of persons equally possible for actual existence. When we have said this there seems nothing left to ask, and all difficulties vanish. For in regard to that great and ultimate question why it has pleased God to choose him among so great a number of possible persons, it is surely unreasonable to demand more than the general reasons which we have given. The reasons in detail surpass our ken. Therefore, instead of postulating an absolute decree, which being without reason would be unreasonable, and instead of postulating reasons which do not succeed in solving the difficulties and in turn have need themselves of reasons, it will be best to say with St. Paul that there are for God's choice certain great reasons of wisdom and congruity which he

follows, which reasons, however, are unknown to
mortals and are founded upon the general order,
whose goal is the greatest perfection of the world.
This is what is meant when the motives of God's
glory and of the manifestation of his justice are
spoken of, as well as when men speak of his mercy,
and his perfection in general; that immense vastness
of wealth, in fine, with which the soul of the same
St. Paul was to thrilled.

XXXII. Usefulness of these principles in matters of piety and of religion.

In addition it seems that the thoughts which we
have just explained and particularly the great principle of the perfection of God's operations and the
concept of substance which includes all its changes
with all its accompanying circumstances, far from
injuring, serve rather to confirm religion, serve to
dissipate great difficulties, to inflame souls with a
divine love and to raise the mind to a knowledge
of incorporeal substances much more than the
present-day hypotheses. For it appears clearly
that all other substances depend upon God just as
our thoughts emanate from our own substances;
that God is all in all and that he is intimately united
to all created things, in proportion however to their
perfection; that it is he alone who determines them
from without by his influence, and if to act is to
determine directly, it may be said in metaphysical
language that God alone acts upon me and he alone
causes me to do good or ill, other substances contributing only because of his determinations;
because God, who takes all things into considera-

tion, distributes his bounties and compels created beings to accommodate themselves to one another. Thus God alone constitutes the relation or communication between substances. It is through him that the phenomena of the one meet and accord with the phenomena of the others, so that there may be a reality in our perceptions. In common parlance, however, an action is attributed to particular causes in the sense that I have explained above because it is not necessary to make continual mention of the universal cause when speaking of particular cases. It can be seen also that every substance has a perfect spontaneity (which becomes liberty with intelligent substances). Everything which happens to it is a consequence of its idea or its being and nothing determines it except God only. It is for this reason that a person of exalted mind and revered saintliness may say that the soul ought often to think as if there were only God and itself in the world. Nothing can make us hold to immortality more firmly than this independence and vastness of the soul which protects it completely against exterior things, since it alone constitutes our universe and together with God is sufficient for itself. It is as impossible for it to perish save through annihilation as it is impossible for the universe to destroy itself, the universe whose animate and perpetual expression it is. Furthermore, the changes in this extended mass which is called our body cannot possibly affect the soul nor can the dissipation of the body destroy that which is indivisible.

XXXIII. Explanation of the relation between the soul and the body, a matter which has been regarded as inexplicable or else as miraculous; concerning the origin of confused perceptions.

We can also see the explanation of that great mystery "the union of the soul and the body," that is to say how it comes about that the passions and actions of the one are accompanied by the actions and passions or else the appropriate phenomena of the other. For it is not possible to conceive how one can have an influence upon the other and it is unreasonable to have recourse at once to the extraordinary intervention of the universal cause in an ordinary and particular case. The following, however, is the true explanation. We have said that everything which happens to a soul or to any substance is a consequence of its concept; hence the idea itself or the essence of the soul brings it about that all of its appearances or perceptions should be born out of its nature and precisely in such a way that they correspond of themselves to that which happens in the universe at large, but more particularly and more perfectly to that which happens in the body associated with it, because it is in a particular way and only for a certain time according to the relation of other bodies to its own body that the soul expresses the state of the universe. This last fact enables us to see how our body belongs to us, without, however, being attached to our essence. I believe that those who are careful thinkers will decide favorably for our principles because of this single reason, viz., that they are able to see in what consists the relation between the soul and the body, a parallelism which appears inexplicable in any other way. We can also see that the perceptions of our senses even when they are clear must necessarily contain certain confused elements, for as all the bodies in the universe are in sympathy, ours receives the impressions of all the others, and while our senses respond to everything, our soul cannot pay attention to every particular. That is why our confused sensations are the result of a variety of perceptions This variety is infinite. It is almost like the confused murmuring which is heard by those who approach the shore of a sea. It comes from the continual beatings of innumerable waves. If now, out of many perceptions which do not at all fit together to make one, no particular one perception surpasses the others, and if they make impressions about equally strong or equally capable of holding the attention of the soul, they can be perceived only confusedly.

XXXIV. Concerning the difference between spirits and other substances, souls or substantial forms; that the immortality which men desire includes memory.

Supposing that the bodies which constitute a *unum per se*, as human bodies, are substances, and have substantial forms, and supposing that animals have souls, we are obliged to grant that these souls and these substantial forms cannot entirely perish, any more than can the atoms or the ultimate elements of matter, according to the position of other philosophers; for no substance perishes, although it may become very different. Such substances also express the whole universe, although more imperfectly than do spirits. The principle difference, however, is that they do not know that they are, nor what they are. Consequently, not being able to reason, they are unable to discover necessary and universal truths. It is also because they do not reflect regarding themselves that they have no moral qualities, whence it follows that undergoing a thousand transformations, as we see a caterpillar change into a butterfly, the result from a moral or practical standpoint is the same as if we said that they perished in each case, and we can indeed say it from the physical standpoint in the same way that we say bodies perish in their dissolution. But the intelligent soul, knowing that it is and having the ability to say that word "I" so full of meaning, not only continues and exists, metaphysically far more certainly than do the others, but it remains the same from the moral standpoint, and constitutes the same personality, for it is its memory or knowledge of this ego which renders it open to punishment and reward. Also the immortality which is required in morals and in religion does not consist merely in this perpetual existence, which pertains to all substances, for if in addition there were no remembrance of what one had been, immortality would not be at all desirable. Suppose that some individual could suddenly become King of China on condition, however, of forgetting what he had been, as though being born again, would it not amount to the same practically, or as far as the effects could be perceived, as if the individual were annihilated, and a king of China were the same instant created in his place? The individual would have no reason to desire this.

XXXV. The excellence of spirits; that God considers them preferable to other creatures; that the spirits express God rather than the world, while other simple substances express the world rather than God.

In order, however, to prove by natural reasons that God will preserve forever not only our substance, but also our personality, that is to say the recollection and knowledge of what we are (although the distinct knowledge is sometimes suspended during sleep and in swoons) it is necessary to join to metaphysics moral considerations. God must be considered not only as the principle and the cause of all substances and of all existing things, but also as the chief of all persons or intelligent substances, as the absolute monarch of the most perfect city or republic, such as is constituted by all the spirits together in the universe, God being the most complete of all spirits at the same time that he is greatest of all beings. For assuredly the spirits are the most perfect of substances and best express the divinity. Since all the nature, purpose, virtue and function of substances is, as has been sufficiently explained, to express God and the universe, there is no room for doubting that those substances which give the expression, knowing what they are doing and which are able to understand the great truths about God and the universe, do express God and the universe incomparably better than do those natures which are either brutish and incapable of recognizing truths, or are wholly destitute of sensation and knowledge. The difference between intelligent substances and those which are not intelligent is quite as great as between a mirror and one who sees. As God is himself the greatest and wisest of spirits

it is easy to understand that the spirits with which
he can, so to speak, enter into conversation and
even into social relations by communicating to
them in particular ways his feelings and his will so
that they are able to know and love their benefac-
tor, must be much nearer to him than the rest of
created things which may be regarded as the instruments of spirits. In the same way we see that all
wise persons consider far more the condition of a
man than of anything else however precious it may
be; and it seems that the greatest satisfaction which
a soul, satisfied in other respects, can have is to see
itself loved by others. However, with respect to
God there is this difference that his glory and our
worship can add nothing to his satisfaction, the
recognition of creatures being nothing but a consequence of his sovereign and perfect felicity and
being far from contributing to it or from causing
it even in part. Nevertheless, that which is reasonable in finite spirits is found eminently in him and
as we praise a king who prefers to preserve the life
of a man before that of the most precious and rare
of his animals, we should not doubt that the most
enlightened and most just of all monarchs has the
same preference.

**XXXVI. God is the monarch of the most perfect re-
public composed of all the spirits, and the happiness of
this city of God is his principal purpose.**

Spirits are of all substances the most capable of
perfection and their perfections are different in this
that they interfere with one another the least, or
rather they aid one another the most, for only the
most virtuous can be the most perfect friends.

Hence it follows that God who in all things has the greatest perfection will have the greatest care for spirits and will give not only to all of them in general, but even to each one in particular the highest perfection which the universal harmony will permit. We can even say that it is because he is a spirit that God is the originator of existences, for if he had lacked the power of will to choose what is best, there would have been no reason why one possible being should exist rather than any other. Therefore God's being a spirit himself dominates all the consideration which he may have toward created things. Spirits alone are made in his image, being as it were of his blood or as children in the family, since they alone are able to serve him of free will, and to act consciously imitating the divine nature. A single spirit is worth a whole world, because it not only expresses the whole world, but it also knows it and governs itself as does God. In this way we may say that though every substance expresses the whole universe, yet the other substances express the world rather than God, while spirits express God rather than the world. This nature of spirits, so noble that it enables them to approach divinity as much as is possible for created things, has as a result that God derives infinitely more glory from them than from the other beings, or rather the other beings furnish to spirits the material for glorifying him. This moral quality of God which constitutes him Lord and Monarch of spirits influences him so to speak personally and in a unique way. It is through this that he humanizes himself, that he is willing to suffer anthropologies, and that he enters into social

relations with us and this consideration is so dear
to him that the happy and prosperous condition of
his empire which consists in the greatest possible
felicity of its inhabitants, becomes supreme among
his laws. Happiness is to persons what perfection
is to beings. And if the dominant principle in the
existence of the physical world is the decree to
give it the greatest possible perfection, the primary
purpose in the moral world or in the city of God
which constitutes the noblest part of the universe
ought to be to extend the greatest happiness possible. We must not therefore doubt that God has
so ordained everything that spirits not only shall
live forever, because this is unavoidable, but that
they shall also preserve forever their moral
quality, so that his city may never lose a person,
quite in the same way that the world never loses a
substance. Consequently they will always be conscious of their being, otherwise they would be open
to neither reward nor punishment, a condition
which is the essence of a republic, and above all of
the most perfect republic where nothing can be
neglected. In fine, God being at the same time
the most just and the most debonnaire of monarchs,
and requiring only a good will on the part of men,
provided that it be sincere and intentional, his subjects cannot desire a better condition. To render them
perfectly happy he desires only that they love him.

**XXXVII. Jesus Christ has revealed to men the mys-
tery and the admirable laws of the kingdom of heaven,
and the greatness of the supreme happiness which God
has prepared for those who love him.**

The ancient philosophers knew very little of these

important truths. Jesus Christ alone has expressed
them divinely well, and in a way so clear and simple that the dullest minds have understood them.
His gospel has entirely changed the face of human
affairs. It has brought us to know the kingdom of
heaven, or that perfect republic of spirits which
deserves to be called the city of God. He it is who
has discovered to us its wonderful laws. He alone
has made us see how much God loves us and with
what care everything that concerns us has been
provided for; how God, inasmuch as he cares for
the sparrows, will not neglect reasoning beings, who
are infinitely more dear to him; how all the hairs of
our heads are numbered; how heaven and earth may
pass away but the word of God and that which
belongs to the means of our salvation will not pass
away; how God has more regard for the least one
among intelligent souls than for the whole machinery of the world; how we ought not to fear those
who are able to destroy the body but are unable to
destroy the soul, since God alone can render the soul
happy or unhappy; and how the souls of the righteous are protected by his hand against all the
upheavals of the universe, since God alone is able
to act upon them; how none of our acts are forgotten; how everything is to be accounted for; even
careless words and even a spoonful of water which
is well used; in fact how everything must result in
the greatest welfare of the good, for then shall the
righteous become like suns and neither our sense
nor our minds have ever tasted of anything
approaching the joys which God has laid up for
those that love him.

CORRESPONDENCE
RELATING TO THE METAPHYSICS.

CORRESPONDENCE RELATING TO THE METAPHYSICS.

I.

Leibniz to Count Ernst von Hessen-Rheinfels.

1/11 Feb., 1686.

. . . Being at a place lately for several days with nothing to do, I wrote out a short discourse on Metaphysics on which I should be very glad to have the opinion of Mons. Arnaud.* For the questions in regard to grace, in regard to the relations of God with created beings, in regard to the nature of miracles, the cause of sin, the origin of evil, the immortality of the soul, ideas, etc., are discussed in a way which seems to offer new points of approach fitted to clear up some great difficulties. I enclose herewith a summary of the articles which it contains, as I have not had time to make a clean copy of the whole.

I therefore beg Your Serene Highness to send him this summary, requesting him to look it over and give his judgment upon it. For, as he excels equally in Theology and in Philosophy, in erudition and in power of thought, I know of no one who is better fitted to give an opinion upon it. I am very desirous to have a critic as careful, as enlightened and as open to reason as is Monsieur Arnaud, being myself also a person the most disposed in the world to submit to reasoning.

---

* Leibniz always used the form *Arnaud.—Trans.*

Perhaps Mons. Arnaud will not find this outline wholly unworthy of his consideration, especially since he has been somewhat occupied in the examination of these matters. If he finds obscurities I will explain myself sincerely and frankly, and if he finds me worthy indeed of his instruction I shall try to behave in such a way that he shall find no cause for being dissatisfied on that point. I beg Your Serene Highness to enclose this with the summary which I am sending and to forward them both to Mons. Arnaud.

SUMMARY OF THE DISCOURSE ON METAPHYSICS

1. Concerning the divine perfection and that God does everything in the most desirable way.

2. Against those who hold that there is in the works of God no goodness, or that the principles of goodness and beauty are arbitrary.

3. Against those who think that God might have made things better than he has.

4. That love for God demands on our part complete satisfaction with and acquiescence in that which he has done.

5. In what the principles of the perfection of the divine conduct consist and that the simplicity of the means counterbalances the richness of the effects.

6. That God does nothing which is not orderly and that it is not even possible to conceive of events which are not regular.

7. That miracles conform to the general order although they go against the subordinate regula-

tions; concerning that which God desires or permits and concerning general and particular intentions.

8. In order to distinguish between the activities of God and the activities of created things, we must explain the conception of an individual substance.

9. That every individual substance expresses the whole universe in its own manner, and that in its full concept is included all its experiences together with all the attendant circumstances and the whole sequence of exterior events.

10. That the belief in substantial forms has a certain basis in fact but that these forms effect no changes in the phenomena and must not be employed for the explanation of particular events.

11. That the opinions of the theologians and of the so-called scholastic philosophers are not to be wholly despised.

12. That the conception of the extension of a body is in a way imaginary and does not constitute the substance of the body.

13. As the individual concept of each person includes once for all everything which can ever happen to him, in it can be seen *a priori* the evidences or the reasons for the reality of each event and why one happened sooner than the other. But these events, however certain, are nevertheless contingent being based on the free choice of God and of his creatures. It is true that their choices always have their reasons but they incline to the choices under no compulsion of necessity.

14. God produces different substances according to the different views which he has of the world and by the intervention of God the appropriate nature of each substance brings it about that what

happens to one corresponds to what happens to all the others without, however, their acting upon one another directly.

15. The action of one finite substance upon another consists only in the increase in the degree of the expression of the first combined with a decrease in that of the second, in so far as God has in advance fashioned them so that they should accord.

16. The extraordinary intervention of God is not excluded in that which our particular essences express because this expression includes everything. Such intervention however goes beyond the power of our natural being or of our distinct expression because these are finite and follow certain subordinate regulations.

17. An example of a subordinate regulation in the law of nature which demonstrates that God always preserves the same amount of force but not the same quantity of motion; against the Cartesians and many others.

18. The distinction between force and the quantity of motion is, among other reasons, important as showing that we must have recourse to metaphysical considerations in addition to discussions of extension, if we wish to explain the phenomena of matter.

19. The utility of final causes in physics.

20. A noteworthy disquisition by Socrates in Plato's Phaedo against the philosophers who were too materialistic.

21. If the mechanical laws depended upon geometry alone without metaphysical influences, the phenomena would be very different from what they are.

22. Reconciliation of the two methods of expla-

nation, the one using final causes and the other efficient causes, thus satisfying both those who explain nature mechanically and also those who have recourse to incorporeal natures.

23. Returning to immaterial substances we explain how God acts upon the understanding of spirits, and ask whether one always keeps the idea of what he thinks about.

24. What clear and obscure, distinct and confused, adequate and inadequate, intuitive and assumed knowledge is, and the definition of nominal, real, causal and essential.

25. In what cases knowledge is added to mere contemplation of the idea.

26. Ideas are all stored up within us. Plato's doctrine of reminiscence.

27. In what respect our souls can be compared to blank tablets and how conceptions are derived from the senses.

28. The only immediate object of our perceptions which exists outside of us is God and in him alone is our light.

29. Yet we think directly by means of our own ideas and not through God's.

30. How God inclines our souls without necessitating them; that there are no grounds for complaint; that we must not ask why Judas sinned because this free act is contained in his concept, the only question being why Judas the sinner is admitted to existence, preferably to other possible persons; concerning the original imperfection or limitation before the fall and concerning the different degrees of grace.

31. The motives for election, faith foreseen, par-

tial knowledge, the absolute decree and that the whole inquiry is reduced to the question why God has chosen and resolved to admit to existence such a possible person whose concept involves such a sequence of gifts of grace and of free acts. This at once overcomes all the difficulties.

32. Applicability of these principles in matters of piety and of religion.

33. Explanation of the inter-relation of soul and body which has been usually considered inexplicable and miraculous; also concerning the origin of confused perceptions.

34. The difference between spirits and other substances, souls or substantial forms, and that the immortality which people wish for includes remembrance.

35. Excellence of spirits; that God considers them preferably to the other created things; that spirits express God rather than the world while other simple substances express rather the world than God.

36. God is the monarch of the most perfect republic which is composed of all the spirits, and the felicity of this city of God is his principal purpose.

37. Jesus Christ has disclosed to men the mystery and the admirable laws of the Kingdom of Heaven and the greatness of the supreme happiness which God has prepared for those who love him.

II

Arnauld to Count Ernst von Hessen-Rheinfels.

March 13, 1686.

I have received, Monseigneur, the metaphysical thoughts which Your Highness sent me from Mr.

Leibniz as a witness of his affection and his esteem for which I am very grateful to him. But I have been so busy ever since that only within the last three days have I been able to read his missive.

And at the present time I have such a bad cold that all that I can do now is to tell Your Highness in a couple of words that I find in his thoughts so many things which frightened me and which if I am not mistaken almost all men would find so startling that I cannot see any utility in a treatise which would be evidently rejected by everybody.

I will instance for example what is said in Article 13: That the individual concept of every person involves once for all everything which will ever happen to him, etc. If this is so, God was free to create or not to create Adam, but supposing he decided to create him, all that has since happened to the human race or which will ever happen to it has occurred and will occur by a necessity more than fatal. For the individual concept of Adam involved that he would have so many children and the individual concepts of these children involved all that they would do and all the children that they would have; and so on. God has therefore no more liberty in regard to all that, provided he wished to create Adam, than he was free to create a nature incapable of thought, supposing that he wished to create me. I am not in a position to speak of this at greater length, but Mr. Leibniz will understand my meaning and it is possible that he will find no difficulties in the consequence which I have drawn. If he finds none, however, he has reason to fear that he will be alone in his position, and were I wrong in this last statement I should be still sorrier.

I cannot refrain from expressing to Your Highness my sorrow at his attachment to those opinions, which he has indeed felt could hardly be permitted in the Catholic Church. The Catholic Church would prohibit his entertaining them, and it is apparently this attachment that has prevented his entering the fold, notwithstanding the fact that Your Highness, if I remember rightly, brought him to recognize that there was no reasonable doubt as to its being the true church.* Would it not be better for him to leave those metaphysical speculations which can be of utility neither to himself nor to others, in order to apply himself seriously to the most important matter he can ever undertake, namely, to assure his salvation, by entering into the Church from which new sects can form only by rendering themselves schismatic? I read yesterday by chance one of Saint Augustine's letters in which he answers various questions that were put forward by a Pagan who showed a desire to become a Christian but who always postponed doing so. He says, at the end, what may be applied to our friend "There are numberless problems which are not to be solved before one has faith and will not be solved in life without faith."

III
Leibniz to Count Ernst von Hessen-Rheinfels.

April 12, 1686.
I do not know what to say to M. A.'s letter, and

---

* Leibniz remarks on the margin of Arnauld's letter: "I have always endorsed this sentiment." Interesting as indicating Leibniz's attitude toward Catholicism.—*Editor.*

I never should have thought that a person whose reputation is so great and so real and from whom we have such excellent Reflections on Morals and Logic would be so precipitate in his judgments. After this instance I am not surprised that some are angry at him. Nevertheless I think it well to be patient at times under the ill humor of one whose merit is extraordinary, provided his acts have no serious results and I believe that a judicious reply may dissipate a prejudice ill-founded. I anticipate this justice in M. A.

Whatever reason, however, I may have for complaint, I desire to suppress all reflections which are not essential to the matter in hand and which might serve to increase the ill-feeling, but I hope he will use the same moderation, in case he has the graciousness to act as my instructor. I am only able to assure him that he is quite mistaken in certain of his conjectures, because people of good sense have judged otherwise regarding my positions, and that notwithstanding their encouragement I have not been over quick in publishing anything upon abstract subjects which are to the taste of few people, inasmuch as the public even has as yet heard almost nothing in regard to certain more plausible discoveries which I made several years ago.

I have written down these Meditations only in order to profit for my own sake by the criticisms of more able thinkers and in order to receive confidence or correction in the investigation of these most important truths. It is true that some persons of intelligence have found my opinions acceptable, but I should be the first to warn them if I thought there were the slightest evil effects from them.

This declaration is sincere, and this will not be the first time that I have profited by the instruction of enlightened persons. This is why I shall assuredly be under great obligations to M. A. in case I merit his having the goodness to deliver me from the errors which he thinks dangerous and of which, I declare it in good faith, I am unable to see the evil. But I hope that he will use moderation, and that he will do me justice, because men deserve at least that no wrong be done to them through precipitate judgments.

He chooses one of my theses to show that it is dangerous. But either I am incapable for the present of understanding the difficulty or else there is none in it. This has enabled me to recover from my surprise and has made me think that M. Arnaud's remarks are the result of misconceptions. I will try therefore to deflect him from that strange opinion, which he conceived a little too hurriedly.

I said in the 13th article of my summary that the individual concept of each person involved once for all, all that would ever happen to him. From that he draws this conclusion that all that happens to any person and even to the whole human race must occur by a necessity more than fatal, as though concepts and previsions rendered things necessary and as though a free act could not be included in the concept or perfect view which God has of the person who performs it. And he adds that perhaps I will not find difficulties in the conclusion which he draws. Yet I have expressly protested in that same article that I do not admit such a conclusion. It must be then either that he doubts my sincerity for which I have given him no grounds or else he has not sufficiently examined that which he controverts. I do not complain as much as it appears I have a right to, because I remember that he was writing at a time when an indisposition did not permit him the liberty of his whole mind, as the letter itself witnesses. And I desire to have him know how much regard I have for him.

He says: "If this is true (that is to say that the individual concept of each person involves once for all all that will ever happen to him), God has not been free to create everything that has since happened to the human race, and all that will happen to it for all eternity must occur through a necessity more than fatalistic." (There is some fault in the copy but I have felt able to amend it as above.) "For the individual concept, Adam, has involved that he should have so many children and the individual concept of each one of these children has involved everything that they would do and all the children that they would have, and so on. There is therefore no more liberty in God regarding all that, supposing that he wished to create Adam, than there is to create a nature incapable of thought, supposing that he wished to create me."

To these last words ought properly to have been added the proof of the consequence but it is quite evident that they confuse *necessitatem ex hypothesi* with absolute necessity. A distinction has always been made between God's freedom to act absolutely and his obligation to act in virtue of certain resolutions already made. He hardly understands the case who does not take the whole into consideration. It is little consonant with God's dignity to conceive of him (with the pretext of assuring his freedom) like certain Socinians, as a human being who forms his resolutions according to circumstances. These maintain that he would be no longer free to create what he found good if his first resolutions in regard to Adam or other men already involved a relationship to that which concerned their posterity. Yet all agree that God has regulated from all eternity the whole course of the universe without this fact diminishing his freedom in any respect. It is clear also that these objectors separate the will-acts of God one from another while his acts are in fact inter-related. For we must not think of the intention of God to create a certain man Adam as detached from all the other intentions which he has in regard to the children of Adam and of all the human race, as though God first made the decree to create Adam without any relation to his posterity. This, in my opinion, does away with his freedom in creating Adam's posterity as seems best to him, and is a very strange sort of reasoning. We must rather think that God, choosing not an indeterminate Adam but a particular Adam, whose perfect representation is found among the possible beings in the Ideas of God and who is accompanied by certain individual circumstances and among other predicates possesses also that of having in time a certain posterity,—God, I say, in choosing him, has already had in mind his posterity and chooses them both at the same time.

I am unable to understand how there is any evil in this opinion. If God should act in any other way he would not act as God. I will give an illustration. A wise prince in choosing a general whose intimates he knows, chooses at the same time certain colonels and captains whom he well knows this general will recommend and whom he will not wish to refuse to him for certain prudential reasons. This fact, however, does not at all destroy the absolute power of the prince nor his freedom. The same applies to God even more certainly.

Therefore to reason rightly we must think of God as having a certain more general and more comprehensive intention which has regard to the whole order of the universe because the universe is a whole which God sees through and through with a single glance. This more general intention embraces virtually the other intentions touching what transpires in this universe and among these is also that of creating a particular Adam who is related to the line of his posterity which God has already chosen as such and we may even say that these particular intentions differ from the general intention only in a single respect, that is to say, as the situation of a city regarded from a particular point of view has its particular geometrical plan. These various intentions all express the whole universe in the same way that each situation expresses the city. In fact the wiser a man is, the less detached intentions does he have, and again the more views and intentions that one has the less comprehensive and inter-related they are.

Each particular intention involves a relation to all the others, so that they may be concerted together in the best way possible. Far from finding in this anything repellent, I think that the contrary view destroys the perfection of God. In my opinion one must be hard to please or else prejudiced when he finds opinions so innocent or rather so reasonable, worthy of exaggerations so strange as those which were sent to Your Highness.

If what I said be thought over a little it will be found to be evident *ex terminis:* for by the individual concept, Adam, I mean of course a perfect representation of a particular Adam who has certain individual characteristics and is thus distinguished from an infinity of possible persons very similar to him yet for all that different from him (as ellipses always differ from the circle, however closely they may approach it). God has preferred him to these others because it has pleased God to choose precisely such an arrangement of the universe, and everything which is a consequence of this resolution is necessary only by a hypothetical necessity and by no means destroys the freedom of God nor that of the created spirits. There is a possible Adam whose posterity is of a certain sort, and an infinity of other possible Adams whose posterity would be otherwise; now is it not true that these possible Adams (if we may speak of them thus) differ among themselves and that God has chosen only one who is precisely ours? There are so many reasons which prove the impossibility, not to say the absurdity and even the impiety of the contrary view, that I believe all men are really of the same opinion when they think over a little what they are saying. Perhaps M. A. also, if he had not been prejudiced against me as he was at first, would not have found my propositions so strange and would not have deduced from them the consequences which he did.

I sincerely think I have met M. Arnaud's objection and I am glad to see that the point which he has selected as the most startling, is in my opinion so little so. I do not know, however, whether I will have the pleasure of bringing M. Arnaud to acknowledge it also. Among the thousand advantages of great intellectual ability there is this little defect, that those who are possessed of this great intellectual ability, having the right to trust to their opinions, are not easily changed. As for myself, who am not of this stamp, I glory in acknowledging that I have been taught, and I should even find pleasure in being taught, provided I could say it sincerely and without flattery.

In addition I wish M. Arnaud to know that I make no pretentions to the glory of being an innovator, as he seems to have understood my opinions. On the contrary I usually find that the most ancient and the most generally accepted opinions are the best. I think that one cannot be accused of being an innovator when he produces only certain new truths without overturning well established beliefs. This is what the Geometers are doing and all those who are moving forward. I do not know if it will be easy to indicate authorized opinions to which mine are opposed. That is why what M. Arnaud says concerning the church has nothing to do with these meditations of mine, and I hope that he does not wish to hold and that he will not be able to prove them to contain anything that can be considered as heretical in any church whatever. Yet if the Church to which he belongs is so prompt to censure, such a proceeding should serve as a notice to be on one's guard. As soon as a person might wish to express some view which would have the slightest bearing

upon Religion and which might go a little beyond
what is taught to children, he would be in danger of
getting into difficulties or at least of having some
church father as a sponsor, which is saying the
same things *in terminis*. Yet even that would not
be perhaps sufficient for complete safety, above all,
when one has no means of support.

If Your Serene Highness were not a Prince whose
intelligence is as great as is his moderation, I should
have been on my guard in speaking of these things.
To whom, however, do they relate better than to
you, and since you have had the goodness to act as
intermediary in this discussion, can we without
imprudence have recourse to any other arbitrator?
In so far as the concern is not so much regarding
the truth of certain propositions as regarding their
consequences and their being tolerated, I do not
believe that you will approve so much vehemence
over so small a matter. It is quite possible, however, that M. A. spoke in those severe terms only
because he believed that I would admit the consequence which he had reason to find so terrifying and
that he will change his language after my explanation. To this, his own sense of justice will contribute as much as the authority of Your Highness.
             I am, with devotion, etc.

IV

Leibniz to Count Ernst von Hessen-Rheinfels.

                              April 12, 1686.
I have received M. Arnaud's verdict and I think
it well to disabuse his mind by the enclosed reply
in the form of a letter to Your Highness. But I

confess that I have had much difficulty in suppress-
ing a desire as much to laugh as to express pity,
inasmuch as the good man seems really to have lost
a part of his mind and seems not to have been able
to keep from crying out against everything as do
those seized with melancholy to whom everything
which they see or think of appears black. I have
shown a good deal of moderation toward him but I
have not avoided letting him quietly know that he
is wrong. If he has the kindness to rescue me
from the errors which he attributes to me and which
he thinks to have seen in my writings, I wish that
he would suppress the personal reflections and the
severe expressions, which I have feigned not to
notice out of the respect which I have for Your
Serene Highness and also because of the respect
which I have for the merits of the good man.

Yet I am surprised at the difference which there
is between our pretended Santons and those persons
of the world who pretend to no such position and have
much more the effect. Your Serene Highness is a
Sovereign Prince and still you have shown to me a
moderation which I wonder at, while M. Arnaud is
a famous theologian whose meditations on religious
subjects ought to have rendered him mild and char-
itable, yet what he says seems often haughty, rough
and full of severity. I am not surprised now that
he has so easily fallen out with Father Malebranche
and others who used to be his fast friends. Father
Malebranche has published writings which M.
Arnaud treated extravagantly almost as he has done
in my case. The world has not always been of his
opinions. He must take care, however, not to
excite his bilious temper. It will deprive us of

all the pleasure and all the satisfaction which I had anticipated in a mild and reasonable debate.

I believe he received my paper when he was in an ill humor and finding himself put to trouble by it, he wanted to revenge himself by a rebuff. I know that if Your Serene Highness had the leisure to consider the objection which he brought forward, you could not refrain from laughing at seeing the slight cause he had for making such tragic exclamations; quite as one would laugh on hearing an orator who should say every few minutes, "O coelum, O terra, O maria Neptuni."

I am glad that there is nothing more repellent, or more difficult in my thoughts than what he objects to. For according to him if what I say is true (namely that the individual concept or consideration of Adam, involves all that will happen to him and to his posterity), it follows that God will have no liberty any longer with respect to the human race. He imagines therefore that God is like a human being who forms his resolves in accordance with circumstances, while on the contrary, God, foreseeing and having regulated all things from all eternity, has chosen from the first the entire sequence and inter-relation of the universe and consequently not simply an Adam but such an Adam in regard to whom he foresaw that he would do such and such things and would have such and such children, without, however, this prevision of God's, though ordained from all time, interfering at all with his freedom. On this point all theologians, excepting some Socinians who think of God as a human being, are agreed. And I am surprised that the desire to find something repellent in my thoughts, prejudice

against which had engendered in his mind a confused and ill-directed idea, has led this learned man
to speak against his own knowledge and convic-
tions. For I am not so unfair as to imitate him
and to impute to him the dangerous doctrine of
those Socinians which destroys the sovereign perfection of God, although he seems almost to incline
to that doctrine in the heat of debate.

Every man who acts wisely considers all the circumstances and bearings of the resolve which he
makes, and this in accordance with the measure of
his abilities. And God, who sees every thing perfectly and with a single glance, can he have failed
to make his plans in conformity with everything
which he saw? And can he have chosen a particular
Adam without considering and having in mind all
that has relations to him? Consequently it is ridiculous to say that this free resolve on God's part
deprives him of his liberty. Otherwise in order to
be free one must need be ever undecided. Such
are the thoughts which are repellent to Mr. Arnaud.
We will see if through their consequences he will
be able to derive something worse from them. Yet
the most important reflection which I have made
in the enclosed is that he himself some time ago
expressly wrote to Your Serene Highness that no
trouble was given to a man who was in their church
or who wished to be in it, for his philosophical
opinions and here is he now, forgetting this moderation, and losing control of himself over a trifle. It
is therefore dangerous to consort with such people
and Your Serene Highness sees how many precau-
tions one should take. This was one of the very
reasons why I communicated the summary to M.

Arnaud, viz., to probe a little and to see what his behaviour would be. But *tange montes et fumigabunt.* As soon as one swings away the least amount from the positions of certain professors they burst forth into explosions and thunders.

I am very positive that the world will not be of his opinion but it is always well to be on one's guard. Perhaps, however, Your Highness will have a chance to let him know that to act in such a way, is to rebuke people unnecessarily, so that henceforth he may use a little more moderation. If I am not mistaken Your Highness had a correspondence with him about the methods of restraint and I should like to learn the results of it.

I may add that milord has now gone to Rome and apparently will not return to Germany so soon as was thought. One of these days I am going to Wolfenbütel and will do my best to recover Your Highness's book. It is said that M. Varillas has written a History of Modern Heresies.

Mastrich's letter which Your Highness communicated to me regarding the conversions of Sedan seems quite reasonable. M. Maimburg, they say, reports that St. Gregory the Great also approved of this principle, namely that one should not trouble himself even if the conversion of Heretics was feigned, provided that thus their children were really gained over. But it is not permitted to kill some persons in order to gain others, although Charlemagne used almost exactly this method against the Saxons, forcing them to accept Religion with the sword at their throats. We have now here a Monsieur Leti who has brought us his History of Geneva in five volumes dedicated to the House of

Brunswick. I do not know what relationship he finds between the two. He says quite good things at times and is a good conversationalist.

I am, etc.

V

Leibniz to Count Ernst von Hessen-Rheinfels.

5/15 April, 1686.

Your Serene Highness will have received the letter which I sent by the preceding post, to which I joined, in the form of a letter to Your Highness, a communication of which a copy could be sent to M. A. I have since thought it would be better to change those words toward the end, beginning "Nevertheless, if the church in which he is be so prompt to censure, such a procedure ought to serve as a notice," etc., as far as the words, "above all, when one has no means of support," lest M. A. may take the opportunity from them to enter into controversial disputes as if the church were being attacked, which is not at all the intention.

In the copy could be put in their place, "least of all in the communion to which M. A. belongs, where the Council of Trent as well as the Popes have been very wisely satisfied with censuring opinions in which there are points manifestly against the faith and against the customs. They have not gone into the philosophic consequences. If it were necessary to listen to these, then in matters of censure Thomists would pass for Calvinists according to the Jesuits, and the Jesuits would be classed as Semipelagians according to the Thomists.

Both would destroy freedom according to Durandus and Father Louys de Dole, and in general every absurdity would pass for atheism because it could be shown to destroy the nature of God."

VI

Arnauld to Leibniz.

May 13, 1686.

I thought that I ought to address myself to you personally to ask pardon for having given you cause to become angry against me, in that I employed too severe terms when I indicated what I thought of one of your positions. But I protest before God that the fault which I committed was not at all the result of prejudice against you, for I have never had cause to have of you other than a most favorable opinion save in the matter of Religion, in which you found yourself fixed through your birth; neither was I in an ill humor when I wrote the letter which has wounded you, nothing being further from my character than the evil disposition which it pleases many people to attribute to me; neither by a too great attachment to my own opinions was I shocked in seeing you hold contrary opinions, for I can assure you that I have meditated so little on these kinds of subjects that I am able to say that my opinions are not at all fully made up.

I beg you, sir, to believe nothing like that about me but to be convinced that what caused my indiscretion was simply that, having been accustomed to write off-hand to His Highness because he is so good as to readily excuse all my faults, I imagined that I could tell him frankly what I was unable to approve of in one of your opinions because I was very sure it would not pass muster and if I had misunderstood your meaning you would be able to correct me without its going any further.

But I hope, sir, that the Prince will be willing to make peace for me and I may engage him in this by using the words which Saint Augustine used on a similar occasion. He had written very harshly against those who thought that God could be seen with the physical eyes, and a Bishop in Africa who held this opinion, having seen this letter which was not at all addressed to him, was seriously offended by it. This necessitated Saint Augustine's employing a common friend to appease the Prelate and I beg you to imagine that I am saying to the Prince for your ears what Saint Augustine wrote to this friend, to be said to the Bishop: *Dum essem in admonendo sollicitus, in corripiendo nimius atque improvidus fui. Hoc non defendo sed reprehendo: hoc non excuso, sed accuso. Ignoscatur, peto; recordetur nostram dilectionem pristinem et obliviscatur offensionem novam. Faciat certe quod me non fecisse succensuit: habeat lenitatem in dandi venia, quam non habui in illa epistola conscribenda.*

I was in doubt whether I ought not to stop here without going again into the question which was the occasion for our falling out, lest there might again escape me some word which could wound you. But I fear, however, that that would be not to have a sufficiently good opinion of your fairness. I will tell you, therefore, in a few words the difficulties which I still have with this proposition: "The individual concept of each person involves, once for all, all that will ever happen to him."

It seems to me to follow from this that the indi-

vidual concept of Adam has involved that he would
have so many children and the individual concept
of each one of these children involves all that they
will do and all the children which they will have
and so on.   Whence I thought that we could infer
that God was free, in so far as the creating or not
creating of Adam, but supposing that he had wished
to create him, all that has since happened to the
human race has come and must come by a fatalistic
necessity or I thought at least that there was no
more freedom in God regarding all that, supposing
that he had wished to create Adam, than there was
not to create a being capable of thinking, supposing he had wished to create me.

It does not appear to me, Monsieur, that, in
speaking thus, I have confused *necessitatem ex
hypothesi* and absolute necessity, for I was all the
time speaking only against the necessity *ex
hypothesi;* what I find strange is, that all human
events should be quite as necessary by a necessity *ex
hypothesi* after this first supposition that God
wished to create Adam, as it is necessary by the
same necessity for there to be in the world a nature
capable of thinking simply because he has wished
to create me.

You say in this connection various things about
God which do not seem to me sufficient to solve my
difficulty.

1. "That a distinction has always been made
between what God is free to do absolutely and what
he is obliged to do by virtue of certain resolutions
already made."   This position is valid.

2. "That it is little consonant with the dignity
of God to conceive of him (under the pretext of

safeguarding his freedom) in the way that the Socinians do, as a man who forms his resolutions according to the circumstances." Such an opinion is very foolish, I grant you.

3. "That the purposes of God, which are all inter-related must not be isolated. Therefore, the purpose of God to create a particular Adam must not be looked at detached from all the others which he has regarding the children of Adam and of the whole human race." To this also I agree, but I cannot yet see how these can serve to solve my difficulty.

For 1. I confess, in good faith, not to have understood that, by the individual concept of each person (for example of Adam), which you say involves, once for all, all that will ever happen to him, you meant this person in so far as he is in the divine understanding instead of simply what he is in himself. For it seems to me that it is not customary to consider the specific concept of a sphere in relation to that which is its representation in the divine understanding but in relation to what it is in itself. I thought it was thus with the individual concept of each person or of everything.

2. It is enough, however, for me to know what you intend, so that I can conform to it, and inquire if that overcomes all the difficulty which I mentioned above. It does not seem to me that it does.

I agree that the knowledge which God had of Adam when he resolved to create him involved what happened to him and what has happened, or will happen, to his posterity; and therefore if we understand in this sense the individual concept, Adam, what you say about it is very true.

I grant also that the purpose which he had in

creating Adam was not detached from that which
he had regarding what would happen to him and in
regard to all his posterity.

But it seems to me, that after all this there still
remains the question (and this is where my difficulty lies) whether the relationship between those
objects (I mean Adam on the one hand and what
will happen to him and to his posterity on the
other), is such through itself, independently of all
the free decrees of God; or, whether it has been
dependent. That is to say, whether it is only in
consequence of the free decrees by which God has
foreordained all that will happen to Adam and to
his posterity that God has known all that will happen
to Adam and to his posterity; or whether there is,
independent of these decrees, between Adam on
the one hand, and what has happened and will happen to him and his posterity on the other, an intrinsic and necessary connection. Unless you mean the
latter I do not see how it can be true when you say,
"that the individual concept of each person involves
once for all, all that which will ever happen to him,"
even if we understand this concept in its relation to
God.

It seems, moreover, that it is this latter which
you do not accept. For I believe you to suppose
that, according to our way of conceiving, possible
things are possible before any free decree of God,
whence it follows that what is involved in the concept of possible things is involved independently of
all God's free decrees. Now you say "that God
has found among possible things a possible Adam,
accompanied by certain individual circumstances,
who, among other predicates, possesses also that of

having in time a certain posterity." There is, therefore, according to you a connection intrinsic, so to speak, and independent of all the free decrees of God; a connection between this possible Adam and all the separate persons of his posterity and not the persons alone, but in general all that must happen to them. It is this, Monsieur, I speak plainly, that is incomprehensible to me. For your meaning seems to be that the possible Adam whom God has chosen preferably to other possible Adams, had a connection with the very same posterity as the created Adam. In either case it is, as far as I can judge, the same Adam considered now as possible and now as created. If this is your meaning then here is my difficulty.

How many men there are who have come into the world only through the perfectly free decrees of God, such as Isaac, Samson, Samuel and many others! Now the fact that God has known them conjointly with Adam is not owing to their having been involved independently of the decrees of God in the individual concept of the possible Adam. It is, therefore, not true that all the individual personages of the posterity of Adam have been involved in the individual concept of the possible Adam since they would then have been thus involved independently of God's decress.

The same can be said of an infinite number of human events which have occurred by the express and particular commands of God, for instance, the Jewish and Christian Religions, and, above all, the Incarnation of the Word of God. I do not see how it can be said that all these are involved in the individual concept of the possible Adam. Whatever is considered as possible must have all that is conceived of under this idea of possibility independently of the Divine decrees.

Moreover, Monsieur, I do not see how, in taking Adam as an example of a unitary nature, several possible Adams can be thought of. It is as though I should conceive of several possible me's; a thing which is certainly inconceivable. For I am not able to think of myself without considering myself as a unitary nature, a nature so completely distinguished from every other existent or possible being that I am as little able to conceive of several me's as to think of a circle all of whose diameters are not equal. The reason is that these various me's are different, one from the other, else there would not be several of them. There would have to be, therefore, one of these me's which would not be me, an evident contradiction.

Permit me, therefore, Monsieur, to transfer to this me what you say concerning Adam and you may judge for yourself if it will hold. Among possible beings God has found in his ideas several me's, of which one has for its predicates, to have several children and to be a physician, and another to live a life of celibacy and to be a Theologian. God, having decided to create the latter, or the present me, includes in its individual concept the living a life of celibacy and the being a Theologian while the former would have involved in its individual concept being married and being a physician. Is it not clear that there would be no sense in such statements, because, since my present me is necessarily of a certain individual nature, which is the same thing as having a certain individual concept, it will be as impossible to conceive of contradictory predicates in the individual concept me, as to conceive of a me different from me? Therefore we must conclude, it seems to me, that since it is impossible for me not to always remain myself whether I marry or whether I live a life of celibacy, the individual concept of my me has involved neither the one nor the other of those two states. Just as we might say that this block of marble is the same whether it be in repose or in a state of movement and therefore neither movement nor repose are involved in its individual concept. This is why Monsieur, it seems to me, that I ought to regard as involved in my individual concept only what is of such a nature that I would no longer be myself if it were not in me, while, on the other hand, everything which is of such a nature that it might either happen to me or not happen to me without my ceasing to be myself, should not be considered as involved in my individual concept; (although, by the ordinance of God's providence, which never changes the nature of things, it could never happen that that should be in me). This is my thought, which, I believe, conforms wholly to what has always been held by all the philospohers in the world.

That which confirms me in this position is the difficulty I experience in believing it to be good philosophy, to seek in God's way of knowing things, what we ought to think out, either from their specific concepts or from their individual concepts. The divine understanding is the measure of the truth of things, *quoad se*, (as far as they are concerned,) but it does not appear to me that, inasmuch as we are in this life, it can be the measure for us, *quoad nos.*

For what do we know at present of God's knowledge? We know that he knows all things and that he knows them all by a single and very simple act, which is his essence. When I say that we know it I mean that we are sure that this must be so. But do we understand it? And ought we not to recognize that however sure we may be that it is so, it is impossible for us to conceive how it can be? Further, are we able to conceive that, although the knowledge of God is his very essence, wholly necessary and immutable, he has, nevertheless, knowledge of an infinity of things which he might not have had because these things might not have been? It is the same in the case of his will which is also his very essence where there is nothing except what is necessary; and still he wills and has willed, from all eternity, things which he would have been able not to will. I find therefore a great deal of uncertainty in the manner in which we usually represent to ourselves that God acts. We imagine that before purposing to create the world he looked over an infinity of possible things, some of which he chose and rejected the others—many possible Adams, each one with a great sequence of persons and events between whom there was an intrinsic connection. And we think that the connection of all these other things with the one of the possible Adams is exactly like that which we know has been between the created Adam and all his posterity. This makes us think that it was that one of all the possible Adams which God chose and that he did not at all wish any of the others. Without however stopping over that which I have already said, namely, that taking Adam for an example of a unitary nature it is as little possible to conceive of several Adams as to conceive of several me's, I acknowledge in good faith that I have no idea of substances purely possible, that is to say, which God will never create. I am inclined to think that these are chimeras which we construct and that whatever we call possible substances, pure possibilities are nothing else than the omnipotence of God who, being a pure act, does not allow of there being a possibility in him. Possibilities, however, may be conceived of in the natures which he has created, for, not being of the same essence throughout, they are necessarily composites of power and action. I can therefore think of them as possibilities. I can also do the same with an infinity of modifications which are within the power of these created natures, such as are the thoughts of intelligent beings, and the forms of extended substance. But I am very much mistaken if there is any one who will venture to say that he has an idea of a possible substance as pure possibility. As for myself, I am convinced that, although there is so much talk of these substances which are pure possibilities, they are, nevertheless, always conceived of only under the idea of some one of those which God has actually created. We seem to me, therefore, able to say that outside of the things which God has created, or must create, there is no mere negative possibility but only an active and infinite power.

However that may be, all that I wish to conclude from this obscurity and from the difficulty of knowing the way that things are in the knowledge of God and of knowing what is the nature of the connection which they have among themselves and whether it is intrinsic or, so to speak, extrinsic—all that I wish to conclude, I say, from this, is that it is not through God, who with respect to us, dwells in inaccessible light, that we should try to find the true concepts either specific or individual of the things we know; but it is in the ideas about them which we find in ourselves.

Now I find in myself the concept of an individual nature since I find there the concept *me*. I have, therefore, only to consult it in order to know what is involved in this individual concept, just as I have only to consult the specific concept of a sphere to know what is involved there. Now I have no other rule in this respect except to consider whether the properties are of such a character that a sphere would no longer be a sphere if it did not have them; such, for instance, as having all the points of its circumference equally distant from the center. Or to consider whether the properties do not affect its being a sphere, as for instance, having a diameter of only one foot while another sphere might have ten, another a hundred. I judge by this that the former is involved in the specific concept of a sphere while the latter, which was the having a greater or smaller diameter, is not at all involved in it.

The same principle I apply to the individual concept me. I am certain, that, inasmuch as I think, I am myself. But I am able to think that I will make a certain journey or that I will not, being perfectly assured that neither the one nor the other will prevent me from being myself. I maintain very decidedly that neither the one nor the other is involved in the individual concept me. "God however has foreseen," it will be said, "that you will make this journey." Granted. "It is therefore indubitable that you will make it." I grant that also. But does that alter anything in the certitude which I have that whether I make it or do not make it I shall always be myself? I must, therefore, conclude that neither the one nor the other enters into my *me*, that is to say, into my individual concept. It is here it seems to me that we must remain without having recourse to God's knowledge, in order to find out what the individual concept of each thing involves.

This, Monsieur, is what has come into my mind regarding the proposition which troubled me and regarding the explanation which you have given. I do not know if I have wholly grasped your thought but such has been at least my intention. The subject is so abstract that a mistake is very easy. I should, however, be very sorry if you had of me as poor an opinion as those who represent me as a hot-headed writer who refutes others only in calumniating them and in purposely misrepresenting their opinions. This is most assuredly not my character. At times I may express my thoughts too frankly. At times also I may fail to grasp the thoughts of others (for I certainly do not consider myself infallible, and such one would have to be in order never to be mistaken), but even if this should be through self-confidence, never would it be that I misstated them purposely; for I find nothing to be so low as the using of chicanery and artifice in differences which may arise regarding matters of doctrine. This even if it should be with persons whom we have no reason otherwise to love, and still more if the difference is between friends. I believe, Monsieur, that you wish indeed that I place you in this latter class. I can not doubt that you do me the honor to love me. You have given me too many marks of it. And, in my behalf, I protest that the very fault for which I beg you once more to pardon me, was only the result of the affection which God has given me for you and of a zeal for your salvation, a zeal which has been by no means moderate.   I am, etc.,

VII

Arnauld to Count Ernst von Hessen-Rheinfels.

May 13, 1686.

I am very sorry, Monseigneur, to have given to Mr. Leibniz cause to become so angry at me. If I had foreseen it, I should have been on my guard against saying so frankly what I thought of one of his metaphysical propositions. But I ought to have foreseen it and I did wrong in employing such severe terms, not against him personally but against his position. Therefore, I have felt myself compelled to beg his pardon for it and I have done it very sincerely in the letter which I have written him and am sending open to Your Highness. It is also from my heart that I pray you to make peace for me and to reconcile me with a former friend of whom I should be very sorry to have made an enemy by my imprudence.

I shall be very glad, however, if the matter rests there and if I shall not be obliged to tell him what I think of his positions, because I am so over-whelmed with so many other occupations that I should have difficulty in convincing him and these abstract subjects require a great deal of application which I can not devote to them on account of the time which it consumes.

I do not know but that I have forgotten to send you an addition to the Apology for the Catholics. I fear lest I may have, because Your Highness has not mentioned it to me. I am accordingly sending it to you to-day with two Memoirs. The Bishop of Namur, whom the Internuncio has appointed judge, has had difficulty in deciding to accept this post, so great is the fear of the Jesuits. But if their power is so great that justice can not be obtained against them in this world, they have reason to fear that God will punish them with so much the more severity in the next. It is a terrible history and a long one, that of this Canon, whose wickedness apparently would be unpunished if he had not rendered himself odious by his conspiracies and his cabals.

This Lutheran minister of whom Your Highness speaks must have good qualities, but it is something incomprehensible and marking an extremely blind prejudice that he can regard Luther as a man destined by God for the Reformation of the Christian religion. He must have a very low idea of true piety to find it in a man like him, imprudent in his speech and so gluttonous in his manner of living. I am not surprised at what this minister has said to you against those who are called Jansenists, since Luther at first put forward extreme propositions against the co-operation of grace and against the freedom of will so far as to give to one of his books the title *De servo arbitrio, Necessitated Will.* Melancthon, some time after, mitigated these propo-

sitions a great deal and since then the Lutherans
have gone over to the opposite extreme so that the
Arminians have nothing stronger to oppose to the
Gummarists than the doctrines of the Lutheran
Church. There is no cause then for astonishment
that the Lutherans of to-day, who occupy the same
positions as the Arminians, are opposed to the disciples of Saint Augustine. For the Arminians are
more sincere than are the Jesuits. They grant that
Saint Augustine is opposed to them in the opinions
which they have in common with the Jesuits but
they do not think themselves obliged to follow him.

What Father Jobert is requiring from new con-
verts gives grounds for hope that those who are con-
verts only in name may return, little by little,
provided that instruction is given them, that they
are edified by good examples, and that the curacies
are filled with good men. But it woud be spoiling
everything to take from them the vernacular trans-
lations of what is said at Mass. It is only such
leniency that can cure them from the aversion that
has been given to them regarding it. Yet we have
not yet been informed of what has been the outcome
of the storm aroused against the *Année Chrétienne,*
about which I wrote to Your Highness some time
ago.

A gentleman named Mr. Cicati, who is in charge
of the Academy at Brussels and who says he is well-
known by Your Highness because he had the honor
to teach the Princes, Your sons, to ride on horse-
back, is acquainted with a German, a very honest
man, who knows French very well and is a good
lawyer, even having had a charge as councillor, and
who has already been employed to take charge of

young Seigneurs. Mr. Cicati thinks that he would
be a very available man for Your grandsons, above
all, when they make their journey in France and
that meanwhile he could render other services to
Your Highness. I thought it couldn't do any harm
to give you this information. It binds you to
nothing and may be of service to you if you think
it best to have somebody with the young Princes—
someone who shall leave them neither day nor night.

Not knowing the characteristics of Mr. Leibniz, I
beg Your Highness to have the above forwarded
along with the letter which I have written him.

VIII

*Remarks upon Mr. Arnaud's letter in regard to my
statement that the individual concept of each person involves, once for all, all that will ever happen to him:*

May, 1686.

"I thought," says Mr. Arnaud, "that we might
infer that God was free either to create or not to
create Adam, but supposing that he wished to create
him, all that has since happened to the human race
was, or all which will happen is by a fatalistic
necessity, or we might infer at least that there was
no more liberty in God, supposing that he once
wished to create Adam, than there was of not
creating a nature capable of thought in case he
wished to create me." I replied at first that a
distinction must be made between absolute and
hypothetical necessity. To this Mr. Arnaud replies
here that he is speaking only of necessity *ex
hypothesi*. After this declaration the argumentation takes a different phase. The words "fatal

necessity" which he used and which are ordinarily understood as an absolute necessity obliged me to make this distinction, which, however, is now uncalled for, inasmuch as M. Arnaud does not insist upon the fatalistic necessity. He uses alternative phrases; "by a fatalistic necessity or at least, etc."

It would be useless to dispute in regard to the word. In regard to the matter, however, M. Arnaud still finds it strange for me to maintain "that all human events occur by necessity *ex hypothesi* after this single presupposition that God wished to create Adam." To which I have two replies to give. The one is, that my supposition is not merely that God wished to create an Adam whose concept was vague and incomplete but that God wished to create a particular Adam sufficiently determined as an individual. This complete individual concept, in my opinion, involves the relation to the whole sequence of things—a position which ought to appear so much the more reasonable, because M. Arnaud grants here the inter-connection among the resolutions of God, that is to say, that God, having resolved to create a certain Adam, takes into consideration all the resolutions which he will form concerning the whole sequence of the universe; almost in the same way that a wise man who forms a resolution in regard to one part of his plan, has the whole plan in view and will make resolutions better in proportion as he is able to plan for all the parts at the same time.

The other reply is that the sequence, in virtue of which events follow from the hypothesis, is indeed always certain, but that it is not always necessary by a metaphysical necessity, as is that instance which is found in M. Arnaud's example: that God, resolving to create me, could not avoid creating a nature capable of thought. The sequence is often only physical and presupposes certain free decrees of God, as, for instance, do consequences which depend on the laws of motion or which depend upon the following principle of morality—namely, that every mind will pursue that which appears to it the best. It is true that when the supposition of the decrees which produce the consequence is added to the first supposition which constituted the antecedent, namely, God's resolution to create Adam—it is true, I say, that if all these suppositions or resolutions are regarded as a single antecedent, then the consequence follows.

As I have already touched upon these two replies somewhat in my letter sent to the Count, M. Arnaud brings forward answers to them here which must be considered. He acknowledges in good faith that he understood my opinion as if all the events happening to an individual were deducible from his individual concept in the same manner and with the same necessity as the properties of the sphere may be deduced from its specific concept or definition, and as though I had considered the concept of the individual in itself, without regard to the manner in which it is present in the understanding or will of God. "For," he says, "it seems to me that it is not customary to consider the specific concept of a sphere in relation to its representation in the divine understanding but in relation to what it is in itself, and I thought that it was thus with the individual concept of each person."

But, he adds, that now, since he knows what my thought is, it is enough for him to conform to it in inquiring if it overcomes all the difficulties. Of this, he is still doubtful.

I see that M. Arnaud has not remembered, or at least, has not adhered, to the position of the Cartesians who maintain that God, by his will, establishes the eternal truths such as are those regarding the properties of the sphere. But, as I share their opinion no more than does M. Arnaud, I will simply say why I believe that we must philosophize differently in the case of an individual substance from our way of philosophizing in the case of a specific concept of the sphere. It is because the concept of space relations involves only eternal or necessary truths but the concept of an individual involves *sub ratione possibilitatis* that which is in fact or which has relation to the existence of things and to time, and consequently it depends upon certain free decrees of God considered as possible. Because the truths of fact or of existence depend upon the decrees of God. Furthermore, the concept of the sphere in general is incomplete or abstract, that is to say we consider only the essence of the sphere in general or theoretically without regard to the particular circumstances, and consequently the concept does not involve that which is required for the existence of a certain sphere. The concept of the sphere which Archimedes had put upon his tomb is complete and should involve all that pertains to the subject of this thing. That is why in individual or practical considerations, where singulars are dealt with, in addition to the form of the sphere there enters the material of which it is made, the time, the place, and the other circumstances which, by a continual network, would finally involve the whole sequence of the universe, provided we were able to follow out all that these concepts involve. For the concept of this bit of matter out of which this sphere is made, involves all the changes which it has undergone and which it will some day undergo.

In my opinion each individual substance always contains the traces of what has ever happened to it and marks of that which will ever happen to it. What I have just said, however, may suffice to justify my line of thought.

Now, M. Arnaud declares that in taking the individual concept of a person in relation to the knowledge which God had of it when he resolved to create it, what I have said regarding this concept is very true, and he grants also that the will to create Adam was not at all detached from God's will in regard to whatever has happened both to him and to his posterity. He now asks if the connection between Adam and the events occurring to his posterity is dependent or independent of the free decrees of God. "That is to say," as he explains, "whether it is only in consequence of the free decrees by which God has ordained all that will happen to Adam and to his posterity that God has known what will happen to them, or whether, independently of these decrees there is between Adam and the events aforesaid, an intrinsic and necessary connection."

He does not doubt that I would take the second alternative and, in fact, I am unable to take the first in the manner in which he has just explained it. But there seems to me to be a mean position. He proves that I ought to choose the latter because I consider the individual concept of Adam as possible when I maintain that among an infinity of possible concepts God has selected a certain Adam, while the possible concepts in themselves do not at all depend upon the free decrees of God.

But here I must needs explain myself a little better. I say, therefore, that the connection between Adam and human events is not independent of all the free decrees of God, but also, that it does not depend upon them in such a way that each event could happen or be foreseen only because of a particular primitive decree made about it. I think that there are only a few primitive free decrees regulating the sequence of things which could be called the laws of the universe and which, being joined to the free decree to create Adam, bring about the consequences. In very much the same way as but few hypotheses are called for to explain phenomenon. I will make this clearer in what follows.

As regards the objection that possibles are independent of the decrees of God I grant it of actual decrees (although the Cartesians do not at all agree to this), but I maintain that the possible individual concepts involve certain possible free decrees; for example, if this world was only possible, the individual concept of a particular body in this world would involve certain movements as possible, it would also involve the laws of motion, which are the free decrees of God; but these, also, only as possibilities. Because, as there are an infinity of possible worlds, there are also an infinity of laws, certain ones appropriate to one; others, to another, and each possible individual of any world involves in its concept the laws of its world.

The same can be said of miracles, or of the

extraordinary operations of God. These are a part of the general order and conform to the principal purposes of God and consequently, are involved in the concept of this universe, which is a result of these designs. Just as the idea of a building results from the purposes or plans of him who undertakes it, so the idea or concept of this world is a result of the designs of God considered as possible. For everything should be explained by its cause and of the universe the cause is found in the purposes of God. Now, each individual substance, in my opinion, expresses the whole universe, according to a certain aspect and consequently it also expresses the so-called miracles. All this ought to be understood in regard to the general order, in regard to the plans of God, in regard to the sequences of this universe, in regard to the individual substance and in regard to miracles, whether they are taken in the actual condition or whether they are considered *sub ratione possibilitatis.* For another possible world would have all such orderings, according to its own manner, although the plans of ours were preferred.

It can be seen also from what I have just said concerning the plans of God and concerning the primitive laws, that this universe has a certain primary or primitive concept, from which the particular events are only the consequences—with the exception of liberty and contingencies, whose certitude, however, is not affected, because the certitude of events is based in part upon free acts. Now every individual substance of this universe expresses in its concept the universe into which it has entered. Not only the supposition that God has resolved to create this Adam but also any other individual substance that may be, involves the resolves for all the rest, because this is the nature of an individual substance, namely, to have so complete a concept that from it may be deduced all that can be attributed to it, and even the whole universe, because of the inter-connection between things; nevertheless, to speak more strictly, it must be said that it is not so much because God has resolved to create this Adam that he made all his other resolutions, but because the resolution which he made in regard to Adam, as also that which he made in regard to other particular things, are consequences of the resolve which he made in regard to the whole universe and to the principal designs which determine its primary concept; these resolves have established this general and unchangeable order to which everything conforms without even excepting the miracles which are doubtless conformable to the principal designs of God, although the particular regulations which are called the laws of Nature are not always observed.

I have said that the supposition from which all human events can be deduced is not simply that of the creation of an undetermined Adam but the creation of a particular Adam, determined to all the circumstances, chosen out of an infinity of possible Adams. This has given M. Arnaud opportunity to object, not without reason, that it is as little possible to conceive several Adams, understanding Adam as a particular nature, as to conceive of several me's. I agree, but yet, in speaking of several Adams, I do not take Adam for a determined individual. I must, therefore, explain. This is what I meant. When we consider in Adam a part of his predicates, for example, that he was the first man, put into a garden of enjoyment, and that, from his side, God took a woman, and, if we consider similar things, conceived *sub ratione generalitatis* (that is to say, without mentioning Eve or Paradise, or the other circumstances which constitute his individuality), and if we call the person to whom these predicates are attributed Adam, all this does not suffice to determine the individual, for there might be an infinity of Adams, that is to say, of possible persons to whom these would apply who would, nevertheless, differ among themselves. Far from disagreeing with M. Arnaud, in what he says against the plurality of the same individual, I would myself, employ the idea to make it clearer that the nature of an individual should be complete and determined. I am quite convinced in regard to what St. Thomas has taught about intelligences, and what I hold to be a general truth, namely, that it is not possible for two individuals to exist wholly alike, that is, differing *solo numero*. We must, therefore, not conceive of a vague Adam or of a person to whom certain attributes of Adam appertain when we try to determine him, if we would hold that all human events follow from the one presupposition, but we must attribute to him a concept so complete that all which can be attributed to him may be derived from his. Now, there is no ground for doubting that God can form such a concept or, rather, that he finds it already formed in the region of possibilities, that is to say, in his understanding.

It follows, also, that if he had had other circumstances, this would not have been our Adam, but another, because nothing prevents us from saying that this would be another. He is, therefore, another. It indeed appears to us that this block of marble brought from Genoa would be wholly the same if it had been left there, because our senses cause us to judge only superficially, but in reality, because of the inter-connection of things, the universe, with all its parts, would be wholly different and would have been wholly different from the very commencement if the least thing in it happened otherwise than it has. It is not because of their inter-connection that events are necessary, but it is because they are certain after the choice which God made of this possible universe whose concept contains this sequence of things. I hope that what I am about say will enable M. Arnaud himself to agree to this.

Let a certain straight line, A B C, represent a certain time, and let there be a certain individual substance, for example, myself, which lasts or exists during this period. Let us take then, first, the me which exists during the time A B, and again the me which exists during the time B C. Now, since people suppose that it is the same individual substance which perdures, or that it is the me which exists in the time A B while at Paris and which continues to exist in the time B C while in Germany, it must needs be that there should be some reason why we can veritably say that I perdure, or, to say, that the me which was at Paris is now in Germany, for, if there were no reason, it would be quite right to say that it was another. To be sure, my inner experience convinces me *a posteriori* of this identity but there must be also some reason *a priori*. It is not possible to find any other reason, excepting that my attributes of the preceding time and state, as well as the attributes of the succeeding time and state are predicates of the same subject; *insunt eidem subjecto.* Now, what is it to say that the predicate is in the subject if not that the concept of the predicate is found in some sort involved in the concept of the subject? Since from the very time that I began to exist it could be said of me truly that this or that would happen to me, we must grant that these predicates were principles involved in the subject or in my complete concept, which constitutes the so-called me, and which is the basis of the interconnection of all my different states. These, God has known perfectly from all eternity. After this I think that all doubts ought to disappear, for when I say that the individual concept of Adam involves all that will ever happen to him I mean nothing else than what the philosophers understand when they say that the predicate is contained in the subject of true propositions. It is true that the consequences of so clear a teaching are paradoxical, but it is the fault of the philosophers who have not sufficiently followed out perfectly clear notions.

Now I think that M. Arnaud, discerning and fair as he is, will not find my proposition so strange and, although he may not be able to approve of it entirely, yet I almost flatter myself with having his approbation. I agree with what he judiciously has added, in regard to the care that must be employed in having recourse to knowledge of divine things for the determination of what we should decide concerning the concepts of mundane things. But if properly understood, what I have just said must be said even when we speak of God only as much as is necessary. For, even if we should not say that God, in considering Adam, whom he resolved to create, saw all the events which will happen to him, it is enough that we can always prove that he had a complete concept of this Adam which involved these events. Because all the predicates of Adam, either depend upon the other predicates of the same Adam, or they do not. Putting one side those which depend upon others, we have only to gather together all the primitive predicates in order to form a concept of Adam sufficiently complete to deduce whatever will happen to him in so far as a reason is needed. It is evident that God can discover, and indeed effectively conceive such a concept sufficient to assign a reason to all the phenomena pertaining to Adam; but not less clear is it, however, that this concept is possible in itself. Truly, we must not submerge ourselves more than necessary, when we investigate, in divine knowledge and will, because of the great difficulties which there are there. Nevertheless, we may explain what we have derived for our question from such a source without entering into those difficulties which M. Arnaud mentions; for instance, the difficulty of understanding how the simplicity of God is reconcilable with certain things which we are obliged to distinguish from it. It is also very difficult to explain perfectly how God has knowledge which he was able not to have, that is, the knowledge of prevision, for, if future contingencies did not exist, God would have no vision of them. It is true that he might have simple knowledge of future contingencies which would become prevision when joined to his will so that the difficulty above would be reduced to the difficulties present in conceiving of the will of God. That is to say, the question how God is free to will. This, without doubt, passes our ken, but it is not essential to understand it in order to solve our question.

In regard to the manner in which we conceive that God acts when he chooses the best among several possibilities, M. Arnaud has reason to find some obscurity. He seems, nevertheless, to recognize that I am inclined to think that there are an infinity of possible first men, each one with a great sequence of personages and events, and that God chose among them the one which pleased him, together with his sequence. This is not, therefore, so strange as it appears at first. It is true, M. Arnaud says he is inclined to think that substances which are purely possible are only chimeras. In regard to this, I do not wish to dispute, but I hope that, nevertheless, he will grant me as much as I have need of. I agree that there is no other reality in pure possibilities than what they have in the divine understanding, and we see, therefore, that M. Arnaud will be obliged himself to have recourse to the divine knowledge in order to explain them, while he seems above to have wished that they might be sought in themselves. When I grant further what M. Arnaud is convinced of and what I do not deny, that we conceive nothing as possible excepting through the ideas which are actually found in the things which God has created, this does not at all injure my position, for, in speaking of possibilities, I am content if true propositions may be formed concerning them. For example, if there were no perfect square in the world, we should, nevertheless, see that no contradiction was implied in the idea. If we wish to reject absolutely the pure possibles, contingencies will be destroyed, because if nothing is possible except what God has actually created then what God has actually created would be necessary in case he resolved to create anything.

Finally, I agree that in order to determine the concept of an individual substance it is good to consult the concept which I have of myself, just as the specific concept of the sphere must be consulted in order to determine its properties. Nevertheless, there is a great difference in the two cases for the concept of myself and of any other individual substance, is infinitely more extended and more difficult to understand than is a specific concept like that of a sphere which is only incomplete. It is not sufficient that I feel myself as a substance which thinks; I must also distinctly conceive whatever distinguishes me from all other spirits. But of this I have only a confused experience.

Therefore, although it is easy to determine that the number of feet in the diameter is not involved in the concept of the sphere in general, it is not so easy to decide if the journey which I intend to make is involved in my concept; otherwise, it would be as easy for us to become prophets as to be Geometers. I am uncertain whether I will make the journey but I am not uncertain that, whether I make it or no, I will always be myself. Such human previsions are not the same as distinct notions or distinct knowledge. They appear to us undetermined because the evidences or marks which are found in our substance are not recognizable by us. Very much as those who regard sensations merely, ridicule one who says that the slightest movement is communicated as far as matter extends, because experience alone could not demonstrate this to them. When, however, they consider the nature of motion and matter they are convinced of it. It is the same here when the confused experience, which one has of his individual concept in particular, is consulted. He does not take care to notice this inter-connection of events, but, when he considers general and distinct notions which enter into them, he finds the connection. In fact, when I consult the conception which I have of all true propositions, I find that every necessary or contingent predicate, every past, present, or future, predicate, is involved in the concept of the subject, and I ask no more.

I think, indeed, that this will open to us a means of reconciliation. For, I think, that M. Arnaud disliked to grant this proposition, only because he understood the connection which I held to, both as intrinsic and necessary at the same time, while I hold it indeed as intrinsic but not at all as necessary. I have now sufficiently explained that it is founded upon free decrees and free acts. I mean no other connection between the subject and the predicate than that which there is in the most contingent of true propositions. That is to say, I mean that there is always something to be conceived of in the subject which serves to give the reason why this predicate or event pertains to it or why a certain thing *has* happened to it rather than not.

These reasons of contingent truths, however, bring about results without necessitation. It is therefore true that I am able not to make this journey, but it is certain that I will make it. This predicate or event is not connected certainly with my other predicates conceived of incompletely or *sub ratione generalitatis;* but it is certainly connected with a complete individual concept because I presuppose that this concept is constructed expressly in such a way that from it may be deduced all that happens to me. This concept is found doubtless *a parte rei* and is properly a concept of myself which I find under different conditions, since it is this concept àlone that can include them all.

I have so much deference for M. Arnaud and such a good opinion of his judgment, that I easily give up my opinions or at least my expressions as soon as I see that he finds something objectionable in them. It is for this reason that I have carefully followed the difficulties which he put forward and now, after I have attempted to meet them in good faith, it seems to me that I am still not far from those very positions.

The proposition which we are discussing is of great importance and should be firmly established, since from it follows that every soul is a world by itself, independent of everything excepting God; that it is not only immortal, and, so to speak, permanent, but that it bears in its substance traces of everything that happens to it. From it can be deduced also in what the inter-activities of substances consist and particularly the union of soul and body. This inter-activity is not brought about according to the usual hypothesis of the physical influence of one substance upon another because every present state of a substance comes to it spontaneously and is only a sequence of its preceding state. No more is the inter-activity accounted for by the hypothesis of occasional causes as though God intervened differently for ordinary events than when he preserved every substance in its course; and as though God whenever something happened in the body aroused thoughts in the soul which would thus change the course that the soul would itself have taken without this intervention. The inter-activity is in accordance with the hypothesis of concomitants which, to me, appears demonstrative. That is to say, each substance expresses the whole sequence of the universe according to the view or relation that is appropriate to it. Whence it follows that substances agree perfectly and when we say that one acts upon another, we mean that the distinct expression of the one which is acted upon diminishes, but of the one which acts, augments, conformably to the sequence of thoughts which its concept involves. For, although each substance expresses everything, we are justified in attributing to it ordinarily only the expressions which are most evident in its particular relation.

Finally, I think after this, that the propositions contained in the abstract sent to M. Arnaud will appear not only more intelligible but, perhaps, better founded and more important than might have been thought at first.

IX

Leibniz to Arnauld.

Hanover, July 14, 1686.

Monsieur:

As I have great deference for your judgment, I was glad to see that you moderated your censure after having seen my explanation of that proposition which I thought important and which appeared strange to you: "That the individual concept of each person involves once for all, all that will ever happen to him." From this at first you drew this consequence, namely, that from the single supposition that God resolved to create Adam, all the rest of the human events which happened to Adam and to his posterity would have followed by a fatalistic necessity, without God's having the freedom to make a change any more than he would have been able not to create a creature capable of thought after having resolved to create me.

To which I replied, that the designs of God regarding all this universe being inter-related conformably to his sovereign wisdom, he made no resolve in respect to Adam without taking into consideration everything which had any connection with him. It was therefore not because of the resolve made in respect to Adam but because of the resolution made at the same time in regard to all the rest (to which the former involves a perfect relationship), that God formed the determination in regard to all human events. In this it seems to me that there was no fatalistic necessity and nothing contrary to the liberty of God any more than there is in this generally accepted hypothetical necessity which God is under of carrying out what he has resolved upon.

You accept, M., in your reply, this inter-relation of the divine resolves which I put forward and you even have the sincerity to acknowledge that at first you understood my proposition wholly in a different sense, "Because it is not customary for example" (these are your words), "to consider the specific concept of a sphere in relation to its representation in the Divine understanding but in relation to that which it is itself." And you thought "that it was thus also with respect to the individual concept of each person."

On my part, I thought that complete and comprehensible concepts are represented in the divine understanding as they are in themselves but now that you know what my thought is, you say it is sufficient to conform to it and to inquire if it removes the difficulty. It seems then that you realize that my position as explained in this way, to mean complete and comprehensive concepts such as they are in the divine understanding, is not only innocent but is, indeed, right, for here are your words, "I agree that the knowledge which God had of Adam when he resolved to create him involved everything that has happened to him and all that has happened and will happen to his posterity, and therefore, taking the individual concept of Adam in this sense, what you say is very certain." We will go on to see very soon in what the difficulty which you still find consists. Yet I will say one word in regard to the cause for the difference which there is here between concepts of space and those of individual substances, rather in relation to the divine will than in relation to the simple understanding. This difference is because the most abstract specific concepts embrace only necessary or eternal truths which do not depend upon the decrees of God (whatever the Cartesians may say about this whom it seems you have not followed at this point), but the concepts of individual substances which are complete, and sufficient to identify entirely their

subjects and which involve consequently truths that
are contingent or of fact, namely, individual circumstances of time, of space, etc.—such substances, I say,
should also involve in their concept taken as possible, the free decrees or will of God, likewise taken
as possible, because these free decrees are the principal sources for existences or facts while essences
are in the divine understanding before his will is
taken into consideration.

This will suffice to make clearer all the rest and to
meet the difficulties which still seem to remain in
my explanation. For you continue in this way:
"But it seems that after that the question still
remains, and here is my difficulty, whether the connection between these objects, I mean Adam and
human events, is such, of itself, independently of
all the free decrees of God or if it is dependent upon
them. That is to say, whether God knows what
will happen to Adam and his posterity only because
of the free decrees by which God has ordained all
that will happen to them, or if there is, independently of these decrees, between Adam on the one
hand and that which has happened to him and will
happen to him and to his posterity on the other, an
intrinsic and necessary connection." It seems to
you that I will take the latter alternative because I
have said, "That God has found among the possibilities an Adam accompanied by certain individual
circumstances and who, among other predicates, has
also this one of having in time a certain posterity." Now you suppose that I agree that the
possibilities are possible before all the free decrees
of God; supposing, therefore, this explanation of
my position according to the latter alternative, you

think that it has insurmountable difficulties. For there are, as you say with good reason, "an infinity of human events that happen by the expressly particular ordinances of God. Among others, the Jewish and Christian religions and, above all, the Incarnation of the divine word. And I do not know how one could say that all this (which has happened by the free decrees of God), could be involved in the individual concept of the possible Adam. Whatever is considered as possible ought to have everything that could be conceived as being under this concept, independently of the divine decrees."

I wish to state your difficulty exactly, Monsieur, and this is the way in which I hope to satisfy it entirely to your own taste. For it must needs be that it can be resolved, since we cannot deny that there is truly a certain concept of Adam accompanied by all its predicates and conceived as possible, which God knew before resolving to create him, as you have just admitted. I think, therefore, that the dilemma of the alternative explanation which you have proposed may have a mean, and the connection which I conceive of between Adam and human events is intrinsic but it is not necessarily independent of the free decrees of God because the free decrees of God taken as possible enter into the concept of the possible Adam, and when these same decrees become actual they are the cause of the actual Adam. I agree with you, in opposition to the Cartesians, that the possibles are possible before all the actual decrees of God, but the decrees themselves, must be regarded also as possibles. For the possibilities of the individual or of contingent truths involve in their concept the possibility of their causes, that is to say, the free decrees of God in which they are different from generic possibilities or from eternal truths. These latter depend solely upon the understanding of God without presupposing any will, as I have explained it above.

This might be enough, but in order to make myself better understood, I will add that I think there were an infinity of possible ways of creating the world according to the different plans which God might have formed and that each possible world depends upon certain principal plans or designs of God that are his own; that is to say, upon certain primary free decrees conceived *sub ratione possibilitatis*, or upon certain laws of the general order of this possible universe with which they agree and whose concept they determine. At the same time, they determine the concepts of all individual substances which ought to enter into this same universe. Everything, therefore, is in order even including miracles, although these latter are contrary to certain subordinate regulations or laws of nature. Thus, all human events cannot fail to happen as they have actually happened, supposing that the choice of Adam was made. But this is so, not so much because of the concept of the individual Adam, although this concept involves them, but because of the purposes of God, which also enter into this individual concept of Adam and determine the concept of the whole universe. These purposes determine, consequently, as well the concept of Adam as the concepts of all the other individual substances of this universe, because each individual substance expresses the whole universe, of which it is a part according to a certain relation, through the connection which there is between all things, and this connection is owing to the connection of the resolutions or plans of God.

I find that you bring forward another objection, Monsieur, which does not depend upon the consequences, apparently contradicting freedom, as was the objection which I just met, but which depends upon the matter itself and upon the idea which we have of an individual substance. Because, since I have the idea of an individual substance, that is to say of myself, it seems to you that we must seek what is meant by an individual concept in this idea and not in the way in which God conceives of individuals; and just as I have only to consult the specific concept of the sphere in order to decide if the number of feet in the diameter is not determined by this concept, in the same way you say I find clearly in the individual concept which I have of myself that I will be myself, in either case whether I make or do not make the journey which I intend.

In order to make my reply clear, I agree that the connection of events, although it is certain, is not necessary, and that I am at liberty either to make or not to make the journey, for, although it is involved in my concept that I will make it, it is also involved that I will make it freely. And there is nothing in me of all that can be conceived *sub ratione generalitatis*, whether of essence or of specific or incomplete concepts from which it can be deduced that I will make it necessarily. While, on the other hand, from the fact that I am a man, the conclusion can be drawn that I am capable of thinking, and consequently, if I do not make this journey, this will be against no eternal or necessary truth. Still, since it is certain that I will make it there must be indeed some connection between the me which is the subject, and the carrying out of the journey, which is the predicate. The concept of the predicate is always in the subject of a true proposition. There is, therefore, an omission, if I do make it, which will destroy my individual or complete concept, or which would destroy what God conceives or conceived in regard to me even before resolving to create me. For this concept involves, *sub ratione possibilitatis*, the existences or the truths of fact or the decrees of God upon which the facts depend.

I agree, also, that in order to determine the concept of an individual substance it is good to consult that which I have of myself, as we must consult a specific concept of a sphere in order to determine its properties. Nevertheless, there is between the two cases a great difference, for the concept of myself in particular and of any other individual substance is infinitely more extensive and more difficult to understand than is a specific concept, such as a sphere, which is only incomplete and does not involve all the practically necessary circumstances to get at a particular sphere. It is not enough in order to understand what the me is that I am sensible of a subject which thinks, I must also conceive distinctly of all that which distinguishes me from other possible spirits and of this latter I have only a confused experience. Therefore, it is easy to determine that the number of feet in the diameter is not involved in the notion of the sphere in general, it is not so easy to determine certainly, although we can decide quite probably whether the voyage which I intend to make is involved in my concept; were it not so it would be as easy to be a prophet as to be a geometer. Nevertheless as experience is unable to make me recognize a great number of insensible things in the body in regard to which the general consideration of the nature of bodies and of movements might convince me; in the same way, although experience cannot make me feel all that is involved in my concept, I am able to recognize in general that everything which pertains to me is involved in it through the general consideration of an individual concept.

Surely since God can form and does actually form this complete concept which involves whatever is sufficient to give a reason for all the phenomena that happen to me, the concept is therefore possible. And this is the true complete concept of that which I call the me. It is in virtue of this concept that all my predicates pertain to me as to their subject. We are, therefore, able to prove it without mentioning God, except in so far as it is necessary to indicate my dependence. This truth is expressed more forcefully in deriving the concept which is being examined from the divine cognizance as its source. I grant that there are many things in the divine knowledge which we are unable to comprehend but it does not seem to me that we must needs go into them to solve our question. Besides, if, in the life of any person, and even in the whole universe anything went differently from what it has, nothing could prevent us from saying that it was another person or another possible universe which God had chosen. It would then be indeed another individual. There must then be some reason *a priori* independent of my existence why we may truly say that it was I who was at Paris and that it is still I and not another who am now in Germany and consequently it must be that the concept of myself unites or includes different conditions. Otherwise it could be said that it is not the same individual although it appears to be the same and in fact certain philosophers who have not understood sufficiently the nature of substance and of individual beings or of beings *per se* have thought that nothing remained actually the same. It is for this, among other reasons, that I have come to the conclusion that bodies would not be substances if they had only extension in them.

I think, Monsieur, that I have sufficiently met the difficulties regarding the principal proposition, but, as you have made in addition some important remarks in regard to certain incidental expressions, which I used, I will attempt to explain them also. I said that the presupposition from which all human events could be deduced, was not that of the creation of an undetermined Adam but of the creation of a certain Adam determined in all circumstances, selected out of an infinity of possible Adams. In regard to this you make two important remarks, the one against the plurality of Adams and the other against the reality of substances which are merely possible. In regard to the first point, you say with good reason that it is as little possible to think of several possible Adams, taking Adam for a particular nature, as to conceive of several me's. I agree, but in speaking of several Adams I do not take

Adam for a determined individual but for a certain person conceived *sub ratione generalitatis* under the circumstances which appear to us to determine Adam as an individual but which do not actually determine him sufficiently. As if we should mean by Adam the first man, whom God set in a garden of pleasure whence he went out because of sin, and from whose side God fashioned a woman. All this would not sufficiently determine him and there might have been several Adams separately possible or several individuals to whom all that would apply. This is true, whatever finite number of predicates incapable of determining all the rest might be taken, but that which determines a certain Adam ought to involve absolutely all his predicates. And it is this complete concept which determines the particular individual. Besides, I am so far removed from a pluralistic conception of the same individual that I agree heartily with what St. Thomas has already taught with regard to intelligences and which I hold to be very general, namely, that it is not possible for two individuals to exist entirely alike or differing *solo numero*.

As regards the reality of substances merely possible, that is to say, which God will never create, you say, Monsieur, that you are very much inclined to believe that they are chimeras. To which I make no objection, if you mean, as I think, that they have no other reality than what comes to them in the divine understanding and in the active power of God. Nevertheless, you see by this, Monsieur, that we are obliged to have recourse to the divine knowledge and divine power in order to explain them well. I find very well founded that which you say

afterwards, "That we never conceive of any substance merely as possible except under the idea of
a particular one (or through the ideas understood in
a particular one) of those which God has created."
You say also, "We imagine that, before creating
the world, God looked over an infinity of possible
things out of which he chose certain ones and
rejected the others, certain possible Adams (first
men), each with a great sequence of personages with
whom he has an intrinsic connection; and we suppose that the connection of all these other things
with one of these possible Adams (first men) is
wholly similar to that which the actually created
Adam had with all his posterity.   This makes us
think that it is this one of all the possible Adams
which God has chosen and that he did not wish any
of the others."   In this you seem to recognize that
those ideas, which I acknowledge to be mine (provided that the plurality of Adams and their possibilities is understood according to the explanation
which I have given and that all this is understood
according to our manner of conceiving any order in
the thoughts or the operations which we attribute to
God), enter naturally enough into the mind when
we think a little about this matter, and indeed cannot be avoided; and perhaps they have been displeas-
ing to you, only because you supposed that it was
impossible to reconcile the intrinsic connection
which there would be, with the free decrees of God.
All that is actual can be conceived as possible and
if the actual Adam will have in time a certain posterity we cannot deny this same predicate to this
Adam conceived as possible, inasmuch as you grant
that God sees in him all these predicates when

he determines to create him. They therefore pertain to him. And I do not see how what you say regarding the reality of possibles could be contrary to it. In order to call anything possible it is enough that we are able to form a notion of it when it is only in the divine understanding, which is, so to speak, the region of possible realities. Thus, in speaking of possibles, I am satisfied if veritable propositions can be formed concerning them. Just as we might judge, for example, that a perfect square does not imply contradiction, although there has never been a perfect square in the world, and if one tried to reject absolutely these pure possibles he would destroy contingency and liberty. For if there was nothing possible except what God has actually created, whatever God created would be necessary and God, desiring to create anything would be able to create that alone without having any freedom of choice.

All this makes me hope (after the explanations which I have given and for which I have always added reasons so that you might see that these were not evasions contrived to elude your objections), that at the end your thoughts will not be so far removed from mine as they appeared to be at first. You approve the inter-connection of God's resolutions; you recognize that my principal proposition is certain in the sense which I have given to it in my reply; you have doubted only whether I made the connection independent of the free decrees of God, and this with good reason you found hard to understand. But I have shown that the connection does depend in my opinion upon the decree and that it is not necessary, although it is intrinsic.

You have insisted upon the difficulties which there would be in saying, "If I do not make the journey, which I am about to make, I will not be myself," and I have explained how one might either say it or not. Finally, I have given a decisive reason which, in my opinion, takes the place of a demonstration; this is, that always in every affirmative proposition whether veritable, necessary or contingent, universal or singular, the concept of the predicate is comprised in some sort in that of the subject. Either the predicate is in the subject or else I do not know what truth is.

Now, I do not ask for any more connection here than what is found *a parte rei* between the terms of a true proposition, and it is only in this sense that I say that the concept of an individual substance involves all of its changes and all its relations, even those which are commonly called extrinsic (that is to say, which pertain to it only by virtue of the general inter-connection of things, and in so far as it expresses the whole universe in its own way), since "there must always be some foundation for the connection of the terms of a proposition and this is found in their concepts." This is my fundamental principle, which I think all philosophers ought to agree to, and one of whose corollaries is that commonly accepted axiom: that nothing happens without a reason which can be given why the thing turned out so rather than otherwise. This reason, however, often produces its effects without necessitation. A perfect indifference is a chimerical or incomplete supposition. It has seemed that from the principle above mentioned I draw surprising consequences but the surprise is only because people are not sufficiently in the habit of following out perfectly evident lines of thought.

The proposition which was the occasion of all this discussion is very important and should be clearly established, for from it follows that every individual substance expresses the whole universe according to its way and under a certain aspect, or, so to speak, according to the point of view from which it is regarded; and that a succeeding condition is a consequence, whether free or contingent, of its preceding state as though only God and itself were in the world. Thus every individual substance or complete being is, as it were, a world apart, independent of everything else excepting God. There is no argument so cogent not only in demonstrating, the indestructibility of the soul, but also in showing that it always preserves in its nature traces of all its preceding states with a practical remembrance which can always be aroused, since it has the consciousness of or knows in itself what each one calls his me. This renders it open to moral qualities, to chastisement and to recompense even after this life, for immortality without remembrance would be of no value. This independence however does not prevent the inter-activity of substances among themselves, for, as all created substances are a continual production of the same sovereign Being according to the same designs and express the same universe or the same phenomena, they agree with one another exactly; and this enables us to say that one acts upon another because the one expresses more distinctly than the other the cause or reason for the changes,—somewhat as we attribute motion rather to a ship than to the whole sea; and this with reason, although, if we should speak abstractly, another hypothesis of motion could be maintained, that is to say, the motion in itself and abstracted from the cause could be considered as something relative. It is thus, it seems to me, that the inter-activities of created substances among themselves must be understood, and not as though there were a real physical influence or dependence. The latter idea can never be distinctly conceived of. This is why, when the question of the union of the soul and the body, or of action and of passion of one spirit with regard to another created thing, comes into question, many have felt obliged to grant that their immediate influence one upon another is inconceivable. Nevertheless, the hypothesis of occasional causes is not satisfactory, it seems to me, to a philosopher, because it introduces a sort of continuous miracle as though God at every moment was changing the laws of bodies on the occasions when minds had thoughts, or was changing the regular course of the thinking of the soul by exciting in it other thoughts on the occasion of a bodily movement; and in general as though God was interfering otherwise for the ordinary events of life than in preserving each substance in its course and in the laws established for it. Only the hypothesis of the concomitance or the agreement of substances among themselves therefore is able to explain these things in a manner wholly conceivable and worthy of God. And as this hypothesis alone is demonstrative and inevitable in my opinion, according to the proposition which we have just established, it seems also that it agrees better with the freedom of reasonable creatures than the hypothesis of impressions or of occasional causes. God created the soul from the very start in such a manner that for the ordinary events it has no need of these interventions, and whatever happens to the soul comes from its own being, without any necessity, on its part, of accommodation in the sequence of events to the body, any more than there is of the body's accommodating itself to the soul. Each one follows its laws, the one acts freely, the other without choice, and they accord with one another in the same phenomena. The soul is nevertheless the form of its body, because it expresses the phenomena of all other bodies according to their relation to its own.

It may be surprising, perhaps, that I deny the action of one corporeal substance upon another, when this seems so evident, but, besides the fact that others have already done this, we must also consider that it is rather a play of the imagination than a distinct conception. If the body is a substance and not a mere phenomenon, like a rainbow, nor a being, brought together by accident or by accumulation, like a pile of stones, its essence cannot consist in extension and we must necessarily conceive of something which is called substantial form and which corresponds in some sort to the soul. I have been convinced of this, as it were, in spite of myself, after having held a very different opinion before. But, however much I may approve of the Schoolmen in this general and, so to speak, metaphysical accounting for the basis of bodies, I also hold to the corpuscular theory as it is used in the explanation of particular phenomena, and for these latter nothing is gained by applying the terms, forms and qualities. Nature must always be explained mathematically and mechanically, provided it be kept in mind that the principles or the laws of mechanics and of force do not depend upon mathematical extension alone but have certain metaphysical causes.

After all this I think that now the propositions contained in the abstract which was sent to you will appear not only more intelligible but perhaps tenable and more important than might have been thought at first.

X

Leibniz to Arnauld.

Hanover, July 14, 1686.

Monsieur:

I have always had so much esteem for your well-known ability that even when I thought myself ill-treated by your criticism I made the firm resolve to say nothing but what would express great deference toward you; and now you have had the generosity of making me a restitution with interest, or, rather, with liberality — a kindness which I shall cherish deeply, because it brings the satisfaction of thinking that you are well disposed toward me. When I was obliged to speak a little strongly, in order to defend myself from positions which you thought I held, it was because I disapproved of them extremely and because I thought so much of your approbation, that I was the more sensitive when I saw you imputing them to me. I hope that I have been able as well to justify the truth of my opinions as their harmlessness. This, however, is not absolutely necessary and since error by itself can do injury

neither to piety nor to friendship I shall not defend
myself with the same force; and if in the enclosed
paper I have made a reply to your gracious letter
where you have pointed out very clearly and in a
very instructive manner in what respect my reply
has not yet satisfied you, it is not because I pretend
that you will take the time to examine again my
reasons, for it is easy to see that you have more
important business and these abstract questions
require leisure. But I have made the reply so that
at least you may be able to do so in case, on account
of the unexpected consequences which can be
derived from these abstract notions, you may wish
to divert yourself some day. I would desire this
extremely for my own profit and for the clearing up
of certain important truths contained in my abstract,
whose acceptance on your part or at least the
acknowledgement of whose harmlessness, would be
of great consequence to me. I would wish it, I say,
if I had not learned long since to prefer the public
benefit, which is interested in a wholly different
manner in the way in which your time is expended,
to my own particular advantage, which, however,
would not be by any means small. I have already
experienced this advantage from your letter and I
know well enough that there is hardly any one in
the world who can penetrate more ably into the
heart of the matter and who will be able to shed
more light upon so clouded a subject. It is with
difficulty that I speak of the manner in which you
have been willing to do me justice, M., when I asked
only that you be gracious to me. I am covered with
confusion and I say these words only to indicate to
you how sensible I am of this generosity which is

very instructive to me; this all the more because it is unusual and more than unusual in a mind of the first rank   Such a mind, reputation usually puts on guard, not only against the criticism of others but also against its own.   It is rather I who must ask your pardon, and, as it appears that you have granted me it in advance, I will do my best to acknowledge this goodness, to merit its effects, and to preserve for myself always the honor of your friendship, which should be esteemed as so much the more precious because it leads you to act in accord with such Christian and such noble sentiments.

I am not able to let this occasion pass without speaking to you in regard to certain of my meditations since I had the honor of seeing you.   Among other things I have made quite a number of investigations into jurisprudence and it seems to me that something permanent and useful might be established, quite as much for the sake of having ascertained laws, of which there is a great lack in Germany and perhaps also in France, as also for the establishment of short and good forms of procedure.   For this purpose it is not sufficient to be strict with regard to the terms or the established days and other conditions, as is the case with the laws compiled under the code of Louis; for to suffer a good cause to be lost because of formalities, is in jurisprudence a remedy comparable to that of a surgeon who is continually cutting off arms and legs They say that the King is having work done for the reform of chicanery, and I think that something of importance might be done along this line.

I have also been interested in the subject of mines, because of those which we have in our country; and I have frequently visited them by command of the Prince. I think I have made several discoveries in regard to the formation, not so much of the metals as of those forms in which the metals are found and of certain bodies among which they lie. For example, I have shown the manner of the formation of slate.

Besides this I have gathered together memoirs and titles concerning the history of Brunswick, and recently I read a document regarding the boundaries of the Hildesheim bishopric of the canonized Emperor Henry II., where I was surprised to find these words, "for the safety of his royal wife and child." This seemed to me to be quite contrary to the accepted opinion which would have us believe that he maintained a state of virginity toward his wife, St. Cunigunde.

Besides this I have diverted myself frequently with abstract thoughts in metaphysics and geometry. I have discovered a new method of tangents, which I have had printed in the Journal of Leipsic. You know, that Hudde and later De Sluse developed this matter quite far, but there were two things lacking. The one was that when the unknown term or indeterminate was expressed in fractions and irrationals, these had to be eliminated in order to use their methods, which made the calculation assume an extent and an elaborateness very awkward and often unmanageable; while my method is not encumbered at all with fractions or irrationals. This is why the English have made so much of it. The other fault of the method of tangents is that it does not apply to the lines which Descartes calls mechanical and which I prefer to call transcendental; while my method applies to them just the same, and I can calculate the tangent of the cycloid or of any other line. I claim also to give in general the means of reducing these lines to calculation, and I hold that they must be received into geometry, whatever M. Descartes may say. My reason is that there are analytical problems which are of no degree or whose degree is required; *e.g.*, to cut an angle in the incommensurable ratio of one straight line to another straight line. This problem is neither in plane geommetry nor in solid nor in super-solid geometry, it is, nevertheless, a problem, and for this reason I call it transcendental. Such is also this problem: Solve the following equation: $x^x + x = 30$, where the unknown term x is found also in the exponent and the degree also of an equation is required. It is easy to find here that x is equal to 3 for $3^3 + 3$ or $27 + 3$ makes 30. But it is not always so easy to solve it, above all when the exponent is not a rational number; and we must have recourse to lines or loci which are appropriate to the purpose and which therefore must be admitted into geometry. Now I show that the lines which Descartes would exclude from geometry depend upon equations which transcend algebraic degrees but are yet not beyond analysis, nor geometry. I therefore call the lines, which M. Descartes accepts, *algebraic* because they are of a certain degree in an algebraic equation. The others I call *transcendental*. These I reduce to calculations, and their construction I show either through points or through motion; and, if I might venture to say, I claim to advance analysis thereby *ultra Herculis columnas.*

Regarding the subject of metaphysics I claim to

advance by geometrical demonstrations, positing only two primary truths; to wit, in the first place, the *principle of contradiction*, (for if two contradictories could be true at the same time all reasoning would be useless); and secondly, the principle that *nothing is without reason*, or that every truth has its proof *a priori*, drawn from the meaning of the terms, although we have not always the power to attain this analysis. I reduce all mechanics to a single metaphysical proposition and I have several important propositions in geometric form regarding causes and effects, and the same regarding similitude by my definition of which I easily demonstrate several truths which Euclid proves in a roundabout way.

In addition I cannot approve the custom of those who have recourse to their ideas, when they are at the end of their proofs, and who abuse the principle that every clear and distinct conception is good. For I hold that we must possess the criteria of distinct knowledge And seeing that we often think without ideas, employing in place of the ideas in question, characters whose signification we wrongly suppose ourselves to know, and thus form impossible chimeras, therefore I hold that the criterion of a true idea is that its possibility can be proved, whether *a priori* in conceiving its cause or reason, or *a posteriori* when experience enables us to know that it is actually found in nature. This is why I consider definitions to be real when it is known that the defined is possible; otherwise they are only nominal and cannot be trusted; for if by chance the thing defined implies contradictions, two contradictories can be deduced from the same definition. It is for this reason that you had good cause to insist against Father Malebranche that a distinction must be made between true and false ideas, and that too much confidence must not be placed in the imagination under the pretext of a clear and distinct intellection.

I know no one who is better able than yourself to examine this class of thoughts, particularly those whose consequences lead into theology; few people having the necessary penetration and the broad enlightenment which is called for; and few people having that fairness which you have now displayed toward me. I therefore pray God to lengthen your life and not to deprive us too soon of an ally whose like will not be easily found again.

I am yours, sincerely, Monsieur,

XI

Arnauld to Leibniz.

Sept. 28, 1686.

I thought, M., that I might make use of the liberty which you gave me to take my time in replying to your kindness; and therefore I have put it off, until I had completed a work which I had commenced. I have been a gainer in doing you justice, for there was never anything more honorable or more gracious than the manner in which you received my excuses. So much was not called for to make me resolve to acknowledge in good faith that I am satisfied with the manner in which you have explained what was startling to me at first, regarding the concept of the individual nature.

For no man of honor should have any difficulty in
accepting a truth as soon as it is made known to
him. I have been above all struck by this argument, that in every affirmative true proposition,
necessary or contingent, universal or singular, the
concept of the attributes is comprised in some way
in that of the subject. *Predicatum inest subjecto.*

There remains for me only the difficulty in regard
to the possibility of things and in regard to this way
of conceiving of God as though he had chosen the
universe, which he created, out of an infinity of other
possible universes which he saw at the same time
and which he did not choose to create. But as this
has nothing to do properly with the concept of the
individual nature, and as I should have to meditate
at too great length in order to make clear what I
think about it or rather what I find to object to in
the thoughts of others, because they do not seem to
me to do justice to God's power, you will permit me
to pass over this subject.

I would prefer to ask you to clear up two things
which I find in your last letter. They seem to me
important, but I do not understand them very
well.

The first is as to what you mean by "the hypothesis of the concomitance and of the agreement of
substances among themselves." You claim that by
this means, that which happens in the union of the
soul and the body and in the action or the passion
of a mind with respect to any other created thing,
can be explained. I cannot understand what you
say in explaining this thought, which, according to
you, agrees neither with those who think that the
soul acts physically upon the body and the body

upon the soul, nor with those who think that God alone is the physical cause of these effects, and that the soul and the body are only the occasional causes. You say, "God created the soul in such a way that for the ordinary events it has no need of these changes, and that which happens to the soul arises from its own being without its having to agree with the body in what results, any more than the body does with the soul. Each one follows its laws. The one acting with freedom and the other without choice, they fit in together, one with another, in the same phenomenon." Examples will enable you to make your thought clearer: some one wounds my arm. With regard to my body, this is only a bodily motion but my soul at once has a feeling of pain which it would not have if this had not happened to my arm. The question is, what is the cause of this pain? You deny that my body has acted upon my soul, and that God, on the occasion of this which happened to my arm, immediately produced in my soul the feeling of pain. It must be, therefore, that you think that it is the soul which has formed this feeling in itself and this must be what you mean when you say that, "What happens in the soul on the occasioning of the body arises from its own being." St. Augustine was of this opinion because he thought that bodily pain was nothing else than the grief which the soul had when its body was ill-affected. But what reply can be made to those who object that the soul must therefore have known that its body was ill-affected before it could become sorrowful, while in fact it seems to be the pain which informs the soul that the body is injured.

Let us take another example where the body has some movement on the occasioning of the soul. If I wish to take off my hat, I lift my arm to my head This movement of my arm upward is not at all in line with the ordinary laws of motion. What then is its cause? It is because the spirits, having entered into certain nerves, have stimulated them. But these spirits have not been through their own power determined to enter into these nerves. They had not given to themselves the movements which cause them to enter into these nerves. What has given it to them then? Is it God, who has done it on the occasion of my wishing to lift my arm? This is what the partisans of occasional causes say. It seems that you do not approve of their position. It must, therefore, be our soul itself, but this again it seems that you will not grant, for this would be to act physically upon the body; and you appear to deny that a substance can act physically upon another.

The second thing upon which I should like to be enlightened is your statement, "In order that the body or matter should not be a simple phenomenon, like a rainbow, nor a being brought together by accident or by an accumulation, like a pile of stones, it must not consist merely in extension, and there must needs be something which is called the substantial form and which corresponds in some sort to what is called the soul." There are a good many things to ask upon this point.

1st. Our body and our soul are two substances really distinct. Now, if we put into the body a substantial form aside from this extension, we cannot imagine how there should be two distinct substances, we cannot see therefore that this substantial form has any relation to what we call our soul.

2nd. This substantial form of the body must be either extended and divisible or not-extended and indivisible. If we should say the latter, it would seem to be as indestructible as is our soul; and if we should say the former, it would seem that nothing would be gained toward making the body a *unum per se,* any more than if it consisted only in extension. For it is the divisibility of extension into an infinity of parts which presents the difficulty of conceiving it as a unit. This substantial form therefore would not remedy this difficulty at all so long as it also is divisible like extension itself.

3rd. Is it the substantial form of a block of marble which makes it one? If this is so, what becomes of that substantial form when it ceases to become one, after it has been cut in two? Is it annihilated, or does it become two? The first is inconceivable, if this substantial form is not a mere manner of being, but is a substance; and it cannot be said that it is a manner of being or a mode, because then the substance, of which this form would be the mode, would be an extension. This apparently is not your thought. And if this substantial form should become two instead of one, why would not the same be said of the extended alone without this substantial form?

4th. Do you give to extension a general substantial form such as has been admitted by certain Schoolmen who have called it *formam corporeitatis?* Or do you wish that there should be as many different substantial forms as there are different bodies and are these different in kind when the bodies are different in kind?

5th. In what do you put the unity which is attributed to the earth, to the sun, or to the moon, when we say that there is only one earth which we inhabit, one sun which lightens us, only one moon which turns about the earth in so many days? Do you think that this earth, for example, made up of so many heterogeneous parts must necessarily have a substantial form which is appropriate to it and which gives to it this unity? It does not seem that you believe this. I should say the same thing of a tree, of a horse, and still further I would instance mixtures; for example, milk is composed of the serum, of the cream, and of the portion which hardens. Are there here three substantial forms, or is there only one?

6th. Finally, it will be said that it is not worthy of a philosopher to admit entities of which there are no clear distinct ideas; and there are no such clear and distinct ideas of these substantial forms. And furthermore even, you do not let them be proved by their effects, since you acknowledge that it is by a corpuscular philosophy that all the particular phenomenon of nature should be explained, and that there is no advantage in bringing up these forms.

7th. The Cartesians in order to find unity in bodies have denied that matter was divisible to infinity and they have held that indivisible atoms must be accepted; but I think that you do not share their opinion.

I have examined your little brochure and I find it very subtle, but take care lest the Cartesians should reply that it brings nothing up against their position, because you posit something which they think false —namely, that a stone, in descending, gives to its own self this greater velocity which it acquires as it descends. They will say that this acceleration comes from the corpuscles, which, in rising, cause everything that they find in their way to descend and impart to them a part of the motion which they had; and therefore there is no cause for surprise if the body B, four times the weight of A, has more motion when it has fallen one foot than the body A when it has fallen four feet, because the corpuscles which have pressed upon B have communicated to it a motion proportioned to its mass and those which have pressed upon A, in proportion to its mass. I do not assure you that this reply will be valid, but I think at least that you ought to see if there be anything in it. I shall be very glad to know what the Cartesians have said to your brochure.

I do not know whether you have examined what M. Descartes says in his letters in regard to the general principle of mechanics. It seems to me that when he wishes to show why the same force can lift by means of a machine twice or four times as much as what it can lift without a machine, he declares that he has not taken into consideration the velocity. My recollection about it, however, is very confused, for I have gone into those things only from time to time and at odd moments, and it is more than twenty years since I have seen any of those books.

I do not wish you, M., to turn away from any of your occupations however important, in order to reply to the two objections which I have brought forward. You may do as you please about them and at your leisure.

I should like very much to know if you have not given the finishing touches to the two machines which you invented while at Paris. The one in the province of arithmetic seemed to be much more perfect than that of M. Pascal, and the other was an absolutely correct watch.

I am yours devotedly,

XII

Count Ernst von Hessen-Rheinfels to Leibniz.

Rheinfels, 21/31, Oct., 1686.

Monsieur:

I enclose herewith a letter from M. Arnauld, which, by some carelessness of mine, has been here over two weeks. On account of occupation in other business I have not read it, and besides such matters are too remote and speculative for me. I send you also four other writings that you may be interested in, and remain,

Yours very affectionately,

E.

XIII

Draft of the letter of Nov. 28-Dec. 8 to Arnauld.

The hypothesis of concomitance is a consequence of the conception which I have of substance, for, in my opinion, the individual concept of a substance involves all that will ever happen to it, and it is in this that complete beings differ from those which are not complete. Now, since the soul is an individual substance it must be that its concept, idea, essence or nature involves all that will happen to it, and God, who sees it perfectly, sees there what it will do or endure forever and all the thoughts which it will have. Therefore, since our ideas are only the consequences of the nature of the soul and are born in it by virtue of its concept, it is useless to ask regarding the influence of another particular substance upon it. This aside from the fact that this influence would be absolutely inexplicable. It is true that certain thoughts come to us when there are certain bodily movements and that certain bodily movements take place when we have certain thoughts, but this is because each substance expresses the whole universe in its fashion and this expression of the universe which brings about a movement in the body is perhaps a pain in regard to the soul. It is customary to attribute the action to that substance whose expression is more distinct and which is called the cause, just as when a body is swimming in water there are an infinity of movements of the particles of water in such a way that the place which the body leaves may always be filled up in the shortest way. This is why we say that this body is the cause of the motion, because by its means we can explain clearly what happens. But if we examine the physics and the reality of the motion, it is quite as easy to suppose that the body is in repose and that all the rest is in motion conformably to this hypothesis, since every movement in itself is only relative, that is to say, is a change of position which cannot be assigned to any one thing with mathematical precision; but the change is attributed to that body by means of which the whole is most clearly explained. In fact, if we take all phenomena, great or small, there is only one single hypothesis which serves to explain everything clearly. We can therefore say, that, although this body is not an efficient physical cause of these effects, its idea is at least, so to speak, the final cause of them, or, if you prefer, a model cause* of them in the understanding of God; because, if we wish to ask what reality there is in motion we may imagine that God desires expressly to produce all the changes of position in the universe exactly the same as that ship was producing them while going through the water. Is it not true that it happens exactly in the same way, for it is not possible to assign any real difference? If we speak with metaphysical precision there is no more reason for saying that the ship presses upon the water in order to make that large number of circular movements because of which the water takes the place of the ship, than to say that the water itself exerts pressure to make all these circles and that it therefore causes the ship to move conformably. Unless we say, however, that God expressly desired to produce such a great number of movements so well fitted together, we do not give any real cause for it, and as it is not reasonable to have recourse to divine activity for explaining a particular detail, we have recourse to the ship, notwithstanding the fact that, in the last analysis, the agreement of all the phenomena of different substances comes about only because they are productions of the same cause, that is to say, of God. Therefore, each individual substance expresses the resolves which God made in regard to the whole universe. It is therefore for the same

---

Cause exemplaire in the original.

reason that pain is attributed to changes in the body, because thus we reach something distinct and this is enough for us to produce the phenomena or to prevent them.   In order not to advance anything that is unnecessary, however, I say that we only think, and also that we produce only thoughts, and that the phenomena are only thoughts.   As, however, all our thoughts are not effective and do not serve to produce for us others of a certain nature, and since it is impossible for us to work out the mystery of the universal connection between phenomena, we must pay attention by means of experience to those which have produced thoughts before, and this is the way the senses do and this is what is called external action, outside of us.

The hypothesis of the concomitance or of the agreement of substances among themselves, follows from what I have said regarding each individual substance: that it involves, forever, all the accidents that will happen to it and that it expresses the whole universe in its manner.   Thus whatever is expressed in the body by a movement or by a change of position, is perhaps expressed in the soul by a sense of pain.   Since pains are only thoughts, we must not be surprised if they are the consequences of a substance whose nature it is to think. If it happens constantly that certain thoughts are joined to certain movements, this is because God has created from the very start all substances in such a way that in the sequence, all their phenomena shall correspond without any need for a mutual physical influence.   This latter does not even appear explicable.   Perhaps M. Descartes would rather have accepted this concomitance than the hypothesis of occasional causes, for so far as I know, he has never expressed himself upon the matter. I am pleasantly surprised, M., that St. Augustine, as you say, already held some such view, when he maintained that pain is nothing else than the grief which the soul has when its body is ill disposed. This great man surely thought far into things. The soul, however, feels that its body is ill disposed, not through an influence of the body upon the soul, nor by a particular intervention of God who carries the information, but because it is the nature of the soul to express whatever happens in the body, having been created from the start in such a way that the sequence of its thoughts will agree with the sequence of the movements. The same can be said of the motion of my hand upward. It will be asked what it is that influences the spirits to enter into the nerves of a certain material; I reply that it is as much the impressions made by the objects, in virtue of the ordinary laws of motion, as it is the disposition of the spirits or even of the nerves. By the general inter-agreement of things, however, all these dispositions happen only when there is at the same time in the soul the will to which we have been accustomed to attribute the operation. Thus, the souls change nothing in the ordering of the body nor do the bodies effect changes in the ordering of the souls (and it is for this reason that forms should not be employed to explain the phenomena of nature). One soul changes nothing in the sequence of thought of another soul, and in general one particular substance has no physical influence upon another; such influence would besides be useless since each substance is a complete being which suffices of itself to determine by virtue of its own nature all that must happen to it. Nevertheless, one has good reason to say that my will is the cause of this movement of my arm and that an interruption in the continuity of the matter of my body is the cause of the pain, for the one expresses distinctly what the other expresses more confusedly and the action should be attributed to the substance whose expression is most distinct. The same can be said practically where phenomena are produced. If it is not a physical cause, we can say that it is a final cause or better a model cause, that is to say, that the idea in the understanding of God has contributed to God's resolve in regard to this particularity, when the determination regarding the universal sequence of things was being made.

The second difficulty is incomparably greater regarding the substantial forms and the souls of bodies, and I grant that I am not myself satisfied in regard to it. First of all, we must maintain that the bodies are substances and not merely true phenomena like the rainbow, but, on the other hand, even if this were granted, it might be inferred, I think, that the corporeal substance consists neither in extension nor in divisibility for it will be granted that two bodies distant from each other, for example, two triangles are not really one substance; suppose now that they come together to compose a square, does the mere contact make them one substance? I do not think so. Now, every extended mass may be considered as a composite of two or of a thousand others, and the only extension there is, is that by contact. Consequently, we shall never find a body of which we can say that it is really one substance; it will always be an aggregate of several. Or rather, it will not be a real being, because the component parts are subject to the same difficulty, and we should never reach a real being, for the beings which result from an aggregation have only as much reality as there is in their ingredients. Whence it follows that the substance of a body, if it has one, must be indivisible; whether we call it soul or form makes no difference to me.

The general conception of individual substance, which seems to appeal to you, M., evidences the same thing, that extension is an attribute which can never constitute a complete being; no action can ever be derived from extension, and no change. It merely expresses a present state. Never does it express the future or the past state as the conception of a substance should. When two triangles are joined, we cannot decide how this union is made, for this might happen in several ways, and whatever can have several causes is never a complete being.

Nevertheless, I acknowledge that it is very difficult to answer several question which you have put, I think we must say that if bodies or substantial forms, for example, if the beasts have souls, then these souls are indivisible. This is also the opinion of St. Thomas. Are these souls therefore indestructible? I think they are, unless it is possible that in accordance with the opinion of M. Leeuwenhoeck every birth of an animal is only the transformation of an animal already alive. There is ground, moreover, for thinking that death is also another transformation. The soul of man, however, is something more divine. It is not only indestructible but it always knows itself and continues to exist with self-consciousness. Regarding its origin, it can be said that God produced it only when this animated body, which was in the seed, determined itself to assume human form. This brute soul, which formerly animated this body before the transformation, is annihilated when the reasoning soul takes its place; or if God changes the one into the other by giving to the former a new perfection by means of an extraordinary intervention, this is a particular in regard to which I have not sufficient light.

I do not know whether the body, when the soul or substantial part is put aside, can be called a substance. It might very well be a machine, an aggregation of several substances, of such sort that if I were asked what I should say regarding the *forma cadaveris* or regarding a block of marble, I should say that they might perhaps be units by aggregation, like a pile of stones, but that they are not substances. The same may be said of the sun, of the earth, of machines; and with the exception of man, there is no body, of which I can be sure that it is a substance rather than an aggregate of several substances or perhaps a phenomenon. It seems to me, however, certain, that if there are corporeal substances, man is not the only one, and it appears probable that beasts have souls although they lack consciousness.

Finally, although I grant that the consideration of forms or souls is useless in special physics, it is, nevertheless, important in metaphysics. Just as geometers pay no attention to the composition of the continuum, and physicists do not ask whether one ball pushes another or whether it is God who does this.

It would be unworthy of a philosopher to admit these souls or forms without reason, but without them it is not possible to understand how bodies are substances.

XIV

Leibniz to Arnauld.

Hanover, Nov. 28-Dec. 8, 1686.

Monsieur:

As I have found something very extraordinary in the frankness and in the sincerity with which you accepted certain arguments which I employed, I cannot avoid recognizing it and wondering at it. I was quite confident that the argument, based upon the general nature of propositions, would make some impression upon your mind, but I confess at the same time that there are few people able to enjoy truths so abstract whose cogency, perhaps, no one else would have been able to see so easily. I should like to be instructed by your meditations regarding the possibilities of things. They would certainly be profound and important, inasmuch as they would have to deal with those possibilities in a manner that might be worthy of God. But this will be at your convenience. As regards the two difficulties which you have found in my letter, the one regarding the hypothesis of the concomitance or of the agreement of substances among themselves, the other regarding the nature of the forms of corporeal substances, I grant that the difficulties are considerable, and if I were able to meet them entirely I

should think myself able to decipher the greatest
secrets of universal nature. But *est aliquid prodire
tenus*.

As regards the first I find that you have yourself
sufficiently explained the obscurity that you found
in my statement concerning the hypothesis of concomitance, for, when the soul has a feeling of pain
at the same time that the arm is injured, I think it
is as you say, M., that the soul forms for itself this
pain, which is a natural consequence of its condition
or of its concept. And it is surprising that St.
Augustine, as you have remarked, seems to have
recognized the same thing, when he said that the
pain which the soul has in these accidents is nothing else than a grief which accompanies the ill condition of the body. In fact, this great man has
very stable and profound thoughts. But it will be
asked, how does the soul know this ill condition of
the body? I reply that it is not by any impression
or action of the body upon the soul but because the
nature of every substance carries a general expression of the whole universe and because the nature
of the soul bears more particularly a distincter
expression of that which happens immediately to
its body. This is why it is natural for it to notice
and to recognize the accidents of its body by its own
accidents. The same is true with regard to the
body when it accommodates itself to the thoughts
of the soul, and when I wish to raise my arm it is
exactly at the very moment when everything is
ready in the body for this effect; in such a way that
the body moves in virtue of its own laws; while it
happens, by the wonderful though unfailing agreement of things among themselves, that these laws

work together exactly at the moment that the will is so inclined. God had regard to this in advance when he formed his resolve in regard to this sequence of all the things in the universe. All of this is only the consequence of the concept of an individual substance, which involves all its phenomena in such a way that nothing can happen to its substance that does not come from its own being, conformably, however, to that which happens to another, although the one may act freely and the other without choice. This agreement is one of the best proofs that can be given of the necessity of a substance which shall be the sovereign cause of everything.

I should like to be able to explain as clearly and decisively the other question with regard to the substantial forms. The first difficulty which you point out, M., is that our souls and our bodies are two substances really distinct; therefore, it seems that one is not the substantial form of the other. I reply that in my opinion our body by itself, leaving out of question the soul, the physical body, can be called one substance only by a misuse of terms, just as a machine or a pile of stones might be called one although they are beings only by accumulation. The regular or irregular arrangement does not constitute a substantial unity. Aside from this, the last Lateran council declares that the soul is veritably the substantial form of our body.

Regarding the second difficulty I agree that the substantial form of our body is indivisible and this seems also to be the opinion of St. Thomas. I agree, also, that every substantial form, or, indeed, every substance is indestructible and also ingenerable, which latter was also the opinion of Albertus

Magnus and among the ancients of the author of the book called *De diaeta*, usually attributed to Hippocrates. They can come into being therefore only by an act of creation. I am a good deal inclined to believe that all the births of unreasoning animals, which do not deserve a new act of creation, are only transformations of another animal already living, but at times invisible. Consider for example, the changes which happen to a silk-worm and other like creatures, where nature has disclosed its secrets in certain instances while it conceals them in others. Thus, brute souls would have all been created from the very beginning of the world, in accordance with that fertility of seeds mentioned in Genesis, but the reasoning soul is created only at the time of the formation of its body, being entirely different from the others souls which we know because it is capable of reflection and imitates on a small scale the divine nature.

Thirdly, I think that a block of marble is, perhaps, only a mass of stones and thus cannot be taken as a single substance but as an assembly of many. For, supposing there are two stones, (for example, the diamond of the Grand Duke and that of the Great Mogul), the same collective name could be put for both of them, and we could say that it is a pair of diamonds, although they are very far apart; but, we should not say that these two diamonds compose one substance. Matters of greater or less in this case would make no difference. They might be brought nearer together, even to touching. Yet they would not be substantially one, and if, after they had touched they were joined together by some other body, constructed to prevent their separation—for instance, if they were set in the same ring—all this would make only what is called a unity by accident, for it is as by accident that they are subjected to the same motion. I hold, therefore, that a block of marble is no more a thoroughly single substance than would be the water in a pond with all the fish included, even when all the water and all the fish were frozen; or any more than a flock of sheep, even when the sheep were tied together so that they could only walk in step and so that one could not be touched without producing a cry from all. There is as much difference between a substance and such a being, as there is between a man and a community—say a people, an army, a society or college, which are moral beings, yet they have an imaginary something and depend upon the fiction of our minds. Substantial unity calls for a thoroughly indivisible being, naturally indestructible since its concept involves all that must happen to it. This characteristic cannot be found either in forms or in motions, both of which involve something imaginary as I could demonstrate. It can be found, however, in a soul or a substantial form, such as is the one called the me. These latter are the only thoroughly real beings as the ancients recognized and, above all, Plato, who showed very clearly that matter alone does not suffice for forming a substance. Now, the me above mentioned or whatever corresponds to it, in each individual substance can neither be made nor destroyed by the bringing together or the separation of the parts. Such juxtapositions are wholly apart from the constitution of a substance. I cannot tell exactly whether there are other true corporeal substances beside those which have life. But souls serve to give us a certain knowledge of others at least by analogy.

All this can contribute to clear up the fourth difficulty, for, without bothering with what the Schoolmen have called *formam corporeitatis*, I assign substantial forms to all corporeal substances that are more than mechanically united.

But fifthly, if I am asked in particular what I should say of the sun, the earth, the moon, of the trees, and of similar bodies, and even of the beasts, I am not able to say surely whether they are animated, or at least whether they are substances, or whether they are merely machines or aggregations of several substances, but I am able to say that if there are no corporeal substances such as I claim, it follows that bodies are only true phenomena like the rainbow. For a continuum is not only divisible to infinity, but every particle of matter is actually divided into other parts as different among themselves as were the two diamonds above mentioned. And since this could always be continued, we should never reach anything of which we could say, here is really a being, unless there were found animated machines whose soul or substantial form constituted the substantial unity independently of the external union of contact. And if there are no substantial forms, it follows that with the exception of men there is nothing substantial in the visible world.

Sixthly, since the conception of an individual substance in general, which I have given, is as clear as is the conception of truth, the conception of corporeal substance will be clear also, and consequently that of substantial forms. If, however, this should not be so, we should be obliged to admit a good many things whose knowledge is not so clear and distinct. I hold that the conception of extension is much less clear and distinct; witness the remarkable difficulties found in the composition of the continuum. And it can, indeed, be said that there is no definite and precise form in the body because of the actual subdivision of the parts. With infinite subdivision the body would be doubtless imaginary and a mere appearance, if there was only the material and its modifications. Nevertheless, it is useless to make mention of the unity, the concept, or the substantial forms of bodies when it is a question of explaining the particular phenomena of nature, just as it is useless for Geometers to examine the difficulties of the continuum when they are at work in solving some problem. These things are nevertheless important and worthy of consideration in their place; all the phenomena of the body can be explained mechanically or by the corpuscular philosophy in accordance with certain assumed mechanical principles without troubling oneself as to whether there are souls or not. In the ultimate analysis of the principles of physics and mechanics, however, it is found that these assumed principles cannot be explained solely by the modifications of extension, and the very nature of force calls for something else.

Finally, in the seventh place I remember that M. Cordemoy, in his treatise on the distinction between the body and the soul, in order to save the substantial unity in the body, feels himself obliged to assume atoms or indivisible extended bodies, so as to have something permanent to constitute a simple being; but you rightly concluded, M., that I did not share this opinion. It appears that M. Cordemoy made an approach to the truth, but he did not yet see in what the true notion of a substance consisted and this latter is the key for most important knowledge. The atom, which consists of only an imagined mass with an infinite duration, an idea which I hold conforms no more to the divine wisdom than does a vacuum, cannot contain in itself all its past and future states and much less those of the whole universe.

I come to your observations upon my objection to the Cartesian principle regarding the quantity of motion, and I grant, M., that the acceleration of a body comes from the impulse of some invisible fluid and that it is like a ship which the wind causes to go at first very slowly and then faster; my demonstration, however, is independent of any hypothesis. Without troubling myself at present as to how the body has acquired the velocity which it has, I accept it such as it is, and I say that a body weighing one pound, which has a velocity of two degrees, has twice as much force as a body weighing two pounds which has a velocity of one degree, because it can raise the same weight twice as high. I hold that in distributing the motion between bodies which come into contact, regard must be had, not to the quantity of motion, as is the case in the Cartesian principle, but to the quantity of the force; otherwise, we should obtain perpetual motion in mechanics. For example, suppose that in a square LM a body A goes along the diagonal 1A 2A to strike two equal bodies B and C at the same moment in such a way that at the moment of con-

tact the three centers of these three spheres are
found in an isosceles right triangle, the whole being
in a horizontal plane. Suppose now that the body
A remains at rest after the contact in the place 2A,
and imparts all its force to the bodies B and C. In
this case B would go from 1B to 2B, having the
velocity and direction 1B2B, and C from 1C to 2C,
with the velocity and direction 1C2C. That is to
say, if A takes one
second of time to pass
with uniform motion
from 1A to 2A before
contact, then in one
second after contact B
will pass to 2B, and C
to 2C. The question
is, what is the length
of 1B2B or 1C2C,
which represent the
velocity. I say that

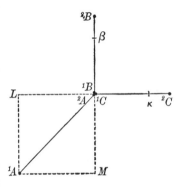

it will be equal to AL or AM sides of the square
LM, for the bodies, being supposed equal, the
forces would be only as the height from which the
body would have to descend in order to acquire
these velocities, that is to say, as the squares of the
velocities. Now, the squares of 1B2B and 1C2C
taken together are equal to the square 1A2A.
Hence, there is as much force after as before the
contact. But we see that the quantity of motion
has been augmented; for, since the bodies are equal,
the quantity of motion can be estimated by their
velocities. Now, before the contact this was the
velocity 1A2A but after the contact it is the
velocity 1B2B plus the velocity 1C2C; 1B2B plus

1C2C, however, is greater than 1A2A; it must needs be, therefore, that, according to M. Descartes, in order to maintain the same amount of motion the body B would go from 1B only to β, or from 1C only to κ, in such a way that 1Bβ or 1Cκ shall each be equal to half 1A2A. In this way, however, there will be as much force lost as the two squares of 1Bβ and of 1Cκ, taken together are less than the square 1A2A.

And, on the other hand, I will show that by another means force can be gained through the contact. For, since according to M. Descartes, the body A with the velocity and direction 1A2A gives by hypothesis to the bodies at rest B and C velocities and directions 1Bβ and 1Cκ so that it may come to rest in their place, reciprocally if these bodies should return and come in contact with the body A resting at 2A with the velocities and directions β1B and κ1C and should come to rest after the contact, they would make A move with the velocity and direction 2A1A. In this way, however, perpetual motion would be inevitably attained for, supposing that the body B, weighing one pound with the velocity β1B could rise to the height of one foot, and C the same, there would be before the shock a force capable of lifting two pounds to the height of one foot, or one pound the height of two feet, but, after the contact of 1B and 1C with 2A the body A weighing one pound and having a double velocity (that is to say, the velocity of 2A1A, double the velocity of β1B or of κ1C), could lift one pound to the height of four feet, for the height to which the bodies can rise by virtue of their velocities is as the squares of their velocities. If, therefore, double the force can be gained, perpetual motion is completely

discovered, or it is possible that force should be
gained or lost, and principles are not well-based
when such consequences can be derived from
them.

I found in Descartes' letters what you mentioned
to me—namely, that he had tried to avoid the consideration of velocities in formulating the reasons
for moving forces and had taken into account only
the heights.   If he had remembered this when he
wrote his principles of physics perhaps he would
have avoided the errors into which he has fallen
with respect to the laws of nature, but he happens to
have avoided the consideration of velocity there
where he might have retained it, and to have retained
it in the case where it could produce errors.   For,
with regard to the power which I call dead (as when
a body makes its first effort to descend before it has
acquired any impetus from the continuance of the
motion), and with regard to the case when two
bodies are in equilibrium (for then, the first efforts
which the one exercises on the other are always
dead), it happens that the velocities are as the distances; when, however, we consider the absolute
force of bodies which have a certain impetuosity
(and this is necessary for establishing the laws of
motion), the calculation should be made from the
cause or from the effect, that is to say, according to
the height to which it can rise by virtue of this
velocity, or according to the height from which it
must descend in order to acquire this velocity.   If
we should attempt to employ the velocity, we should
gain or lose a great deal of force without any reason
for it.   In place of the height we might suppose a
spring or any other cause or effect, and the result

would always be the same; viz., proportional to the squares of the velocities.

I find in The News of the Republic of Letters for the month of September, of this year, that someone named Abbé D. C., of Paris, whom I do not know, has replied to my objection. The trouble is that he seems not sufficiently to have thought over the difficulty. While pretending to contradict me vehemently he grants me more than I wish and he limits the Cartesian principle to the single case of isochronous powers as he calls them, as in the five usual forms of machinery, and this is entirely against Descartes' intention. Besides this, he thinks that the reason why in the case which I proposed one of the bodies has quite as much force as the other although it has a smaller quantity of motion, is the result of this body's having fallen for a longer period since it has come from a greater height. If this made any difference, the Cartesian principle which he wishes to defend would be ruined by that very fact. This reason, however, is not valid, for the two bodies can descend from those different heights in the same time, according to the inclination which is given to the planes along which they must descend; and my objection would still be entirely valid. I hope, therefore, that my objection may be examined by a Cartesian who shall be a Geometer and well versed in these matters.

Finally, M., as I honor you infinitely and am very much interested in whatever concerns you I will be delighted to learn from time to time of the state of your health and of the works which you have in hand; whose value I am proud to be able to recognize. I am, with a passionate zeal,

XV

Leibniz to Count Ernst von Hessen-Rheinfels.
[Taken from my letter of November, 1686.]

I take the liberty, Monseigneur, to beg your Serene Highness to have the enclosed sent to M. Arnaud, and, as it treats of matters far from the external senses and dependent upon pure intellection, which are not agreeable to and most frequently are looked down upon by persons who are, nevertheless, active and successful in the affairs of the world, I will say here something in favor of these meditations; not because I am so fatuous as to wish your Serene Highness to amuse himself with them (this would be as unreasonable as to wish that the general of an army should apply himself to algebra, however important this science may be to any one who is concerned with mathematics), but so that your Serene Highness may better estimate the purpose and the use of such thoughts that might appear unworthy of taking up a man's time; especially since all a man's moments ought to be so precious to him. As these matters are usually treated by the Schoolmen, they are only disputations and distinctions and plays upon words; but there are veins of gold among these barren rocks. I think in fact that thought is the principal and perpetual function of the soul. We shall always think, but we shall not always live here; this is why whatever renders us more capable of thinking about most perfect objects and in the most perfect way is what naturally contributes to our perfection. Nevertheless, the present state of our life compels us to a great number of confused thoughts which do not add to our perfection, such is the knowledge of customs, of genealogies, of languages, and even all historical knowledge of facts, whether civil or natural; these are useful for us in avoiding dangers and in taking care of the bodies and of the men whom we have around us, but they do not enlighten the mind. The knowledge of routes is useful to a traveller while he is on his journey, but whatever has a greater relation to the duties that lie before him *in patria* is more important for him. Now we are destined to live some day a spiritual life, where substances separated from matter will occupy us much more than do the bodies.

Here are a few examples taken from the arts, which will enable us to distinguish between that which enlightens the mind and that which only leads it along as a blind man might be led. If a workman knows by experience or by hearsay that when the diameter is seven feet the circumference of the circle is a little less than twenty-two feet, or if a gunner knows by hearsay, or because he has frequently measured it, that bodies are thrown the farthest at an angle of 45 degrees, the knowledge is confused and is that of an artisan; it does very well for earning a living and for performing services to others, but the knowledge which enlightens the mind is that which is distinct, or which gives the causes or reasons involved, as when Archimedes gave the demonstration for the first rule and Galileo for the second. In a word, it is only knowledge of the reasons in themselves or of the necessary eternal truths, above all of those which are the most comprehensive and which have the most relation to the sovereign being, that are able to make us more perfect. This knowledge alone is good in itself; all the rest is mercenary, and should be learned only when necessary and to serve the needs of this life, and so that this life may be in a better position to contribute afterwards to the perfection of the mind when one's subsistence has been provided for. But the intemperance of men, and what is called the care *de pane lucrando*, and often also vanity, lead us to forget the lord for the valet and the end for the means. This, according to the poet is "to lose the reasons for living while trying to live." Very much as a miser prefers gold to his health, while gold is only for procuring the commodities of life. Now, since that which perfects the mind (leaving aside the light of grace), is the demonstrative knowledge of the greatest truths through their causes or reasons, it must be granted that metaphysics or natural theology which treats of immaterial substances and particularly of God and of the soul, is the most important of all. One cannot go very far in this without inquiring into the true conception of substance, which I, in my preceding letter to M. Arnaud explained in such a manner that he himself who is so exact and who was at first repelled by it, accepted it.

Finally, these meditations furnish surprising consequences which are, nevertheless, of wonderful use in freeing men from doubts regarding the relation of God to created things, his fore-knowledge and fore-ordination and the union of the soul with the body, the origin of evil and other things of this nature. I say nothing here of the great applications that these principles have in the humanities, but at least I am able to say that nothing lifts our minds more to the knowledge and to the love of God, however much nature may help us in this. I confess that all these speculations are of no service without grace and that God gives grace to people who have never dreamed of these meditations, but God wishes also that we should not omit anything on our part and that each one of us according to his vocation and according to the time, should make use of the perfections which God has given to human nature. And since he has created us only that we may know and love him, we cannot work enough toward this nor can we make a better use of our time and of our energy except when we are occupied elsewhere for the public and for the welfare of others.

XVI

Arnauld to Leibniz.

March 4th, 1687.

It has been a long time, M., since I received your letter, but I have been so busy since then that I have not been able to reply to it earlier.

I do not understand very well what you mean by this "distincter expression which our soul bears of that which is now happening to its body," and how it comes about that when someone pricks my finger my soul knows of this pricking before it feels the pain of it. This very "distincter expression," etc., ought to let it know therefore an infinity of other things which happen in my body which, nevertheless, it does not know, for instance all that goes on in the process of digestion and of nutrition.

As for your saying that although my arm raises itself when I wish to raise it, it is not because my soul causes this movement in my arm but it is

because "when I wish to raise it it is exactly at the
very moment when everything is ready in the body
for this very effect, in such a way that the body
moves itself by virtue of its own laws, although it
happens through the wonderful but unfailing agreement of things among themselves that these laws
conspire together at the very same moment that the
will makes its resolution. For God had regard
to this in advance when he resolved upon this
sequence of all the things in the universe." It
seems to me that this is to say the same thing in
other terms that those say who maintain that my
will is the occasional cause for the movement of my
arm and that God is its real cause; for they do not
claim that God does this at the moment by a new
act of will each time that I wish to raise my arm,
but by a single act of the eternal will by which he
has chosen to do everything which he has foreseen
that it will be necessary to do, in order that the universe might be such as he has decided it ought to be.
Does not what you say come to this very thing,
namely that the cause of the movement of my arm
when I wish to lift it is "the wonderful but unfailing
agreement of things among themselves which results
because God had them in mind in advance when he
resolved upon this sequence of all the things in the
universe"? For this forethought of God has not
been able to bring about any event without a real
cause. We must, therefore, find the real cause of
this movement of my arm. You do not wish it to
be my will. I do not think, either, that you believe
a body can move itself or any other body as a real
or efficient cause. There remains therefore only this
"forethought of God," which can be the real and

efficient cause of the movement of my arm. Now you, yourself, called this forethought of God his resolve; and resolve and will are the same thing. Therefore, according to you, every time that I wish to raise my arm, it is the will of God which is the real and efficient cause of this movement.

In regard to the second difficulty, I now understand your position to be very different from what I thought, for I supposed that you would reason thus: the body should be the true substance; now there can be no true substances which have no true unity nor can there be any true unity which has not a substantial form; therefore the essence of a body cannot be its extension, but every body besides its extension should have a substantial form. To this I have replied that a divisible substantial form, such as almost all those who hold to substantial forms understand them, could not give to a body any unity that it did not have without this substantial form.

You agree, but you claim that every substantial form is indivisible, indestructible and ingenerable, being produced only by a real creation; whence it follows:

1st. That every body which can be divided so that each part will remain of the same nature as the whole, such as metals, stones, wood, air, water and the other fluid bodies, have no substantial form.

2nd. That the plants have none, either, since a part of a tree, whether placed in the ground or grafted to another tree, remains a tree of the same sort that it was before.

3rd. That only animals have substantial forms, and that therefore in your opinion only animals are true substances.

4th. And since, as you say, you are not very sure whether brutes have souls or substantial forms, it follows that with the exception of man there is nothing substantial in the visible world, because you claim that substantial unity requires a complete being, indivisible, and through natural means indestructible. This can be found only in a soul or a substantial form like that which I call the Me.

All of this means that every body whose parts are only mechanically united is not a substance but only a machine or an aggregate of several substances.

I will begin with this last. And I will say frankly that it is only a dispute regarding a word. For St. Augustine did not hesitate to recognize that bodies have no real unity; because a unit should be indivisible and no body is indivisible. There is, therefore, no true unity excepting in Spirit, any more than there is a true Me outside of them. Now, what is your conclusion from that? "That there is nothing substantial in those bodies which have no soul or substantial form." In order that this conclusion may be valid we must first of all define substance and substantial in these terms, "I call substance and substantial that which has a true unity." But since this definition has not yet been received there is no philosopher who has not as much right to say, "I call substance that which is not modality or manner of being," and he could therefore maintain that it is untrue to say that there is nothing substantial in a block of marble, "because this block of marble is by no means a manner of being of another substance, and all that can be said of it is that it is not a single substance but several substances joined together mechanically.'' This philosopher would say ''this is what seems to me paradoxical: that there should be nothing substantial in that which seems to be made up of several substances.'' He could add that he understood still less what you meant by the words ''bodies would be without doubt something imaginary and only of appearance if they were composed only of matter and its modifications.'' For you postulate only matter and its modifications in everything that has no soul or no substantial, indestructible, indivisible and ingenerable form and it is only in the case of animals that you admit this class of forms. You will therefore be obliged to say that all the rest of nature is something imaginary and merely an appearance, and for a still stronger reason you would have to say the same thing of all the works of men.

I cannot agree to these latter propositions, but I see no objection to thinking that in every corporeal nature there is only a machine and an aggregate of substances, because of no one of its parts could one say strictly that it is a single substance. This serves merely to make evident what is worth while noticing, as St. Augustine has done, that the substance which thinks, or a spiritual substance, is through this fact much more excellent than extended or corporeal substance. The spiritual substance alone has a true unity and a true ego, while the corporeal substance does not have them. It follows from this, that this fact, that the body has no true unity when its essence is extension, cannot be put forward to prove that extension is not of the essence of the body; for, perhaps, the essence of the body has no true unity, as you grant in the case of all those which are not united to a soul or to a substantial form.

I do not know, M., what inclined you to believe that brutes have these souls or substantial forms, which, according to you, must be indivisible, indestructible and ingenerable. It is not because you consider it necessary to explain their actions, for you say expressly "that all the phenomena can be explained mechanically or by the corpuscular 'philosophy in accordance with certain postulated mechanical principles, without going into the question whether there are souls or not." It is also not because the bodies of brutes need to have a true unity and because they are not mere machines or aggregations of substances; if plants are merely the latter what necessity is there that brutes should be anything else? Further, it is not clear how this opinion can be easily maintained, if we consider these souls as indivisible and indestructible. What would be said of a worm, of which, when cut in two, both parts move off as before? If a house where a hundred thousand silk-worms were being kept should catch fire and burn up, what would become of those one hundred thousand indestructible souls? Would they exist apart from all matter like our souls? In the same way, what became of the souls of those millions of frogs which Moses caused to die when he stopped the plague? And of that innumerable number of quails which the Israelites killed in the desert or of all the animals which perished in the flood? There are also other embarrassing questions in regard to the condition of these souls in each brute at the moment that they are conceived. Is it that they are *in seminibus?* Are they there indivisible and indestructible? *Quid ergo fit, cum irrita cadunt sine ullis conceptibus semina? Quid cum bruta mascula ad foeminas non accedunt toto vitae suae tempore?* It will suffice to have indicated these difficulties.

There still remains the discussion of the unity which a reasoning soul has. It is agreed that it has a true and a perfect unity, a true Me, and that it communicates in some sort this unity and this Me to that composite whole of the soul and body which is called the man; for, although this whole is not indestructible because it perishes when the soul is separated from the body, it is indivisible in this sense, that half a man cannot be conceived of. In considering the body apart, however, in the same way that our soul does not communicate to it its indestructibility, we cannot see, properly speaking, that it communicates either its true unity or its indivisibility. Even though it be united to our soul, nevertheless, its parts are truly united among themselves only mechanically, and thus there is not a single bodily substance, but an aggregation of many corporeal substances. Not less true is it that it is quite as divisible as all the other bodies in nature. The divisibility, however, is inconsistent with unity, therefore it has no true unity. But you say, it acquires the unity through the soul, that is to say, because it belongs to a soul which is a true unit; this, however, is not an intrinsic unity in the body, but is like that of different provinces which are governed by a single king and thus constitute one kingdom.

Although, however, it is true that there is no real

unity except in intelligent natures, each of which
can say the word *Me*, there are, nevertheless, different degrees in this inexact unity which belongs to
bodies; for although there are no bodies which are
not made up of several substances there is, nevertheless, reason for attributing more unity to those
whose parts work together for a similar purpose like
a house or a watch than to those whose parts are only
in contact one with another like a pile of stones or
a bag of coins and only these latter can properly be
called an accidental aggregation. Almost all natural
bodies, which we call one, like a piece of gold, a
star, a planet, are of the first kind; but there are
none which appear to be more so than the organized
bodies, that is, the animals and plants; though there
is no reason to assign souls to them on this account
(and I think also that you assigned none to plants).
For why should not a horse or an orange be considered each one as a complete and whole work quite
as well as a church or a watch? What is essential in
order that a thing may be called one (that is, this
oneness which applies to bodies, but which is very
different from that that applies to spiritual natures)
when the parts are united among themselves only
mechanically as are the parts of the machine? Is
it not the greatest perfection that they can have,
that they are machines so wonderful that only an
all-powerful God could have constructed them?
Our body, considered by itself, is therefore one in
this sense. The relationship, which an intelligent
nature, united to it and governing it, has with it,
may, perhaps, add some unity, but it is not that kind
of unity which pertains to spiritual natures.

I confess, M., that my ideas on the laws of motion

are not clear and distinct enough to enable me to pass judgment upon the difficulty which you have brought up against the Cartesians. The one who replied to you is the Abbé Catelan who has a good mind and is a good geometer; since I left Paris I have not had much intercourse with the philosophers of that country. Inasmuch, however, as you have decided to reply to this Abbé, and as he will perhaps wish to defend his position, it is to be hoped that these discussions will so clear up the difficulty that it will be possible to know which side to take.

I thank you very much for the desire you show to know how I am. I am thankful to say that I am very well for my age, only I had a very bad cold at the beginning of the winter. I am very glad that you are thinking of completing your arithmetical machine. It would be a pity if so fine an invention were lost. I desire greatly, however, that the intention in regard to which you wrote a word to the Prince, who has so much affection for you, may not remain without its effects, for there is nothing towards which a wise man should work with more care and with less of delay than towards what has to do with his salvation. I am, Monsieur,

Your very humble and obedient servant.

A. ARNAULD.

XVII

Leibniz to Arnauld.

Göttingen, April 30, 1687.

Monsieur:

Since I regard your letters as personal benefactions to me and as sincere marks of your liberality, I have no right to ask for them and consequently your reply is never too late. However agreeable and useful they may be to me, I take into consideration what you owe to the public weal and thus suppress my desires. Your criticisms are always instructive and I will take the liberty to go through them in order.

I do not think that there is any difficulty in my saying that "the soul expresses more distinctly, other things being equal, that which pertains to its own body"; since it expresses the whole universe in a certain sense according to the special relation of other bodies to itself, it is not able to express all things equally, otherwise there would be no distinction between souls, but it does not follow from this that the soul should perceive perfectly whatever goes on in the parts of its body, since there are degrees of relationship between these parts themselves and these parts are no more equally expressed than are external things. The greater distance of the latter is made up for by the smallness or by some other hindrance in the internal parts. Thales saw the stars though he did not see the ditch which was at his feet.

The nerves and membranes are for us the parts which are more sensitive than the others and it is, perhaps, only through them that we perceive what seems to happen to the others, because the movements of the nerves, or of the liquids in them, imitate the impressions better and confuse them less, and the most distinct expressions of the soul correspond to the most distinct impressions of the body. Metaphysically speaking, it is not the nerves which act upon the soul, but the one represents the state of the other through the spontaneous relation; it must also be remembered that too many things take place within our bodies to be all separately perceived; we feel only a certain result, to which we are accustomed, and we are not able to distinguish the elements that are involved, because of their multitude. Just as when we hear from afar the sound of the sea, we do not distinguish what each wave does, although each wave has its effect upon our ears. When a striking change happens in our body, we notice it at once and more clearly than the changes outside, which are not accompanied by any special change in our organs.

I do not say that the soul knows the pricking before it has the sense of pain, except as it knows or expresses confusedly all things in accordance with the principles already established. This expression, however, although obscure and confused, which the soul has in advance of the future, is the real cause of that which happens to it and of the clearer conception which it will have later when the obscurity shall have worked out. The future state is only a consequence of the preceding.

I said that God created the universe in such a way that the soul and the body, each acting according to its laws, agree in their phenomena. You think, M., that this coincides with the hypothesis of occasional causes. Were this so I should not be sorry, and I am always glad to find those who hold my positions. I see, however, the reason for your thinking this. You are of the opinion that I would not say a body can move itself, and, the soul not being the real cause either of the motion of the arm or of the body, therefore the cause must be God. My opinion, however, is different. I hold that whatever reality there is in the state which is called motion, may issue quite as well from the bodily substance as the thought and will proceed from the spirit. Everything happens to each substance in consequence of the first state which God gave to it in creating it, and putting aside extraordinary interventions the ordinary agreement consists only in the conservation of the substance itself conformably to its preceding state and to the changes which it carries in itself. Nevertheless, we have the right to say that one body pushes another; that is to say, that one body never begins to have a certain tendency excepting when another which touches it loses proportionately, according to the constant laws which we observe in phenomena; and since movements are rather real phenomena than beings, a movement as a phenomenon is in my mind the immediate consequence or effect of another phenomenon, and the same is true in the minds of others   The condition of one substance, however, is not the immediate consequence of the condition of another particular substance.

I dare not maintain that plants have no souls, nor life, nor any substantial form; since, although one part of a tree planted or grafted can produce a tree of the same kind, it is possible that there is in it a seminal part which already contains a new plant, as it is likely there are living animalcula although very small in the seed of animals which can be transformed into a similar animal; I do not therefore dare to maintain that animals alone are living and endowed with substantial forms. Perhaps there is an infinity of degrees in the forms of corporeal substances.

You say, M., that "those who hold to the hypothesis of occasional causes, saying that my will is the occasional cause, while God is the real cause of the movement of my arm, do not claim that God does this at the moment by a new volition, which he has each time I wish to lift my arm, but through that single act of eternal will, by which he resolved to do everything which he foresaw would be necessary for him to do." To this I reply that we can say with the same reasoning, that miracles also are not the result of a new act of will on God's part, being conformable to a general plan; and I have already stated, in what precedes, that every act of will on God's part involves all the others, but with a certain order of priority; if I properly understand the position of the authors of occasional causes, they introduce a miracle which is not less miraculous for being continual, for it seems to me that infrequency does not constitute the conception of miracle. It will be said that God acts in that, only according to a general rule and consequently without miracle, but I do not grant this consequence and I think that God could make general rules with regard to the miracles themselves. For instance, if God resolved to give his grace immediately, or to perform some other action of this nature every time that a certain condition came about. this action would, nevertheless, be a miracle although quite in the ordinary. I confess that the authors of occasional causes can give another definition of the term, but it seems that according to usage a miracle differs internally and substantially from that which results from ordinary activity, and its distinctiveness does not depend upon its unusualness; properly

speaking, God performs a miracle when he does anything which surpasses the powers which he has given
to created things and which he maintains in them; for
example, if God should make a body, which was
put in circular motion by means of a sling, to go on
freely in a circular line even when it was released
from the attachment, this, when it was neither
pushed nor retained by anything, would be a miracle, for, according to the laws of Nature the body
should travel along the line of the tangent: if, moreover, God should decide that such should always be
the case, he would perform a natural miracle, for
this movement could not be explained by anything
more simple. In the same way, we should have to
say in accordance with the current conception, that
if the continuation of the motion were beyond the
power of bodies, the continuation of the motion
would be a true miracle; while my position is that
the corporeal substance has the power to continue
its changes according to the laws which God has
put into its nature and which he maintains there.

To make myself better understood I will add that
the activities of the mind change nothing at all in
the nature of the body, nor the body in that of
the mind; and I will also add that neither does God
change anything on the occasion of their action
except when he performs a miracle. In my opinion, things are so concerted together that the mind
never desires anything efficaciously excepting when
the body is ready to accomplish it in virtue of its own
laws and forces; while, according to the authors
of occasional causes, God changes the laws of the
body on the occasion of the action of the soul and, *vice
versa*. That is the essential difference between our

positions. Therefore, we should not ask how the soul
can give any motion or new determination to the
animal spirits, since it never does anything of the
kind, for there is no interaction between spirit and
body, and there is nothing which can determine
what degree of velocity a mind will give to a body,
nor what degree of velocity God may be minded to
give to the body on the occasion of the mind's action
according to a certain law.   The same difficulty is
found with regard to the hypothesis of occasional
causes which there is in the hypothesis of a real
influence of the soul upon the body and *vice versa;*
because we can see no relation or basis for such a
rule.   If one were to say, as M. Descartes seems to,
that the soul, or God on the occasion of its acting,
changes merely the direction or determination of the
motion and not the force which is in bodies, (since
it does not seem probable to him that God would
interrupt at each moment on the occasion of the
willing of spirits, this general law of nature,
namely, that the same force should perdure), I
would reply that it will be quite difficult to explain
what connection there can be between the thoughts
of the soul and the sides or the angles of direction of bodies, and furthermore that there is in
nature another general law which M. Descartes has
not perceived but which is, nevertheless, important
—namely, that the sum total of the determinations
or directions must always perdure.   For I find that
if any straight line be drawn, for example, from
east to west, through a given point, and if all the directions of all the bodies in the world in so far as they
advance toward or move away in lines parallel to
this line be calculated, the difference between the

sums of the quantities of all the easterly directions and of all the westerly directions will ever be found the same, whether certain particular bodies which might alone be supposed to have relations among themselves, be regarded or whether the whole universe be regarded. In this latter case the difference is always zero. Everything is perfectly balanced and the easterly and westerly directions in the universe are exactly equal. If God wished to do anything against this principle it would be a miracle.

It is therefore much more reasonable and more worthy of God to suppose that he has created the machinery of the world in such a fashion from the very start, that without doing violence at every moment to the two great laws of nature, that of force and that of direction, but rather by following them exactly, (except in the case of miracles,) it so comes about that the internal springs of bodies are ready to act of themselves, as they should, at the very moment when the soul has a conforming desire or thought. The soul, in turn, has had this desire or thought only conformably to preceding states of the body and thus the union of the soul with the machinery of the body and with the parts which compose it, and the action of the one upon the other consists only in this concomitance, which betokens the wonderful wisdom of the Creator much more than any other hypothesis. It cannot be denied that this at least is possible, and that God is a sufficiently great workman to be able to carry it out; therefore, it can easily be decided that this hypothesis is the most probable, being the simplest and most intelligible and at once avoiding all difficulties; for example, the difficulties involved in criminal actions, where it seems much more reasonable to let God intervene only through the conservation of the created forces.

To employ a comparison, I will say in regard to this concomitance, which I hold to be true, that it is like several bands of musicians or choirs separately taking up their parts and placed in such a way that they neither see nor hear one another, though they nevertheless, agree perfectly in following their notes, each one his own, in such a way that he who hears the whole finds in it a wonderful harmony much more surprising than if there were a connection between the performers. It is quite possible also that a person who is close by one of two such choirs could judge from the one what the other was doing, and would form such a habit (particularly if we supposed that he was able to hear his own choir without seeing it and to see the other without hearing it), that his imagination would come to his aid and he would no longer think of the choir where he was, but of the other, and he would take his own for an echo of the other, attributing to his own only certain interludes, in which certain rules of symphony by which he understood the other did not appear, or else attributing to his own certain movements which he caused to be made from his side, according to certain plans that he thought were imitated by the other because of the inter-relationship which he found in the kind of melody, not knowing at all that those who were in the other choir were doing also something which corresponded according to their own plans.

Nevertheless, I do not at all disapprove of the

statement that minds are in some sort the occasional
and even real causes of certain movements in the
body, for, with regard to the divine resolves, whatever God has foreseen and pre-established with
regard to minds, has been an occasion for his thus
regulating the body from the very start, so that
they might fit in together, each following the laws
and forces that he has given them; and as the state
of one is an unfailing consequence of the other, although frequently contingent and even free, we can
say that God has established a real connection in
virtue of this general conception of substances, which
brings it about that they express one another perfectly. This connection, however, is not immediate,
being founded only upon what God has given them
in creating them.

If my opinion, that substances require a true unity,
is founded only upon a definition which I have
made up contrary to the common usage, this would
be a mere question of words; but besides the fact
that most philosophers have understood this term
in nearly the same way, namely, that "a distinction
should be made between unity through itself and
unity through accident, between substantial form and
accidental form, between an imperfect and a perfect
compound, between natural and artificial," I take
still higher ground and, leaving the question of
terminology, I believe that where there are only
beings by aggregation, there are not even real beings,
because every being by aggregation pre-supposes
beings endowed with true unity, because it obtains its reality only from the reality of the elements of which it is composed, so that it will have
no reality at all if every being of which it is com-

posed is again a being by aggregation; or else we must seek some other foundation for its reality, seeing that by this method it can never be reached, even by searching forever. I grant, M., that in all corporeal nature there exist only machines (some of which are alive), but I do not grant that there exist only aggregations of substances, and if there do exist aggregations of substances it must be that there are also real substances of which all these aggregations are the product; we therefore come necessarily to the mathematical points out of which certain writers have constructed extension, or to the atoms of Epicurus and of M. Cordemoy—things which you reject quite as much as I do; or else we must acknowledge that no reality is to be found in bodies. The other alternative is to say that there are certain substances which have a real unity. I have already said in another letter that the composite of the diamonds of the Grand Duke and of the Great Mogul could be called a pair of diamonds, but this would only be a being of the reason, and if they were brought together they would become a being of the imagination or perception, that is to say, a phenomenon, because contact, common movement and even agreement in design, do not effect a substantial unity. It is true that sometimes there is more and sometimes less basis for supposing that several things constitute one, according as the things have more or less connection, but this is only a means to abbreviate our thinking and to represent the phenomenon.

It seems also that what constitutes the essence of a being by aggregation consists solely in the mode of the being of its component elements. For example, what constitutes the essence of an army? It is simply the mode of being of the men who compose it. This mode of being presupposes, accordingly a substance of which the essence is not a mode of being of a substance. Every machine therefore presupposes some substance in the parts out of which it is made, and there is no plurality without true unities; in short, I consider as an axiom this identical proposition, which receives two meanings only through a change in accent; namely, that what is not truly *a* being is not truly a *being*. It has always been thought that one and being are reciprocal terms. Being is very different from beings, but the plural presupposes the singular; and there where there is no being, are there still less several beings. What can be clearer? I thought, therefore, that I should be permitted to distinguish beings by aggregation from substances, since these beings have their unity only in our minds, and our minds repose upon the relations or the modes of real substances. If a machine is a substance, a circle of men who are holding hands would be one also, so an army, and in fact, any gathering together of substances. I do not say that there is nothing substantial or nothing but appearance in things which have not a true unity, for I acknowledge that they have as much of reality or substantiality as there is of true unity in that which enters into their composition.

You object, M., that it might be of the essence of bodies to have no true unity. But it will be then the essence of bodies to be phenomena deprived of all reality as would be an orderly dream, for phenomena, like the rainbow or like a pile of stones, will be wholly imaginary if they are not com-

posed of beings which have a true unity. You
say that you do not see why I admit substantial
forms or rather corporeal substances endowed with
a true unity. It is because I can conceive of no
reality without a true unity, and in my opinion the
concept of the singular substance involves consequences incompatible with its being a mere aggregation. I can conceive of properties in the substance which cannot be explained by extension, by
form and by motion, quite apart from the fact that
there is no exact and definite *form* in bodies because
of the actual subdivision of the continuum to infinity, and that their *motion* in so far as it is only a
modification of extension and a change of place,
involves something imaginary so that we cannot
determine to which object, among those that change,
it belongs, unless we have recourse to the force that
is the cause of the motion and that inheres in the
corporeal substance. I confess that there is no need
of mentioning these substances and qualities in
explaining particular phenomena, but no more is
there need of inquiring about the intervention of
God, the composition of the continuum, the plenum,
and a thousand other things. The particular events
of nature I confess can be explained mechanically,
but only after having recognized or presupposed the
principles of mechanics. These can be established
a priori only through metaphysical speculations.
The difficulties involved in the composition of the
continuum will never be resolved so long as extension is considered as constituting the substance of
the bodies, and we shall find ourselves entangled
in our own chimeras.

I think furthermore that to attempt to limit true

unity or substance to man alone is as shortsighted in metaphysics as it was in the realm of physics to desire to enclose the world in a sphere. And since true substances are so many expressions of the whole universe taken in a certain sense and so many reduplications of the divine work, it is in conformity with the grandeur and the beauty of the works of God, (seeing that these substances do not clash with one another,) to create in this universe as many of them as is possible and as superior reasons permit. The wholly bare supposition of extension destroys this wonderful variety, since mass, by itself (if we were able to conceive of it), is as much inferior to a substance which is perceptive and which represents the whole universe according to its point of view and according to the impressions or rather relations that its body receives mediately or immediately from all others, as a dead body is below an animal or as a machine is inferior to a man. It is, indeed, through the idea of substance that the evidences of the future are formed in advance and that the traces of the past are preserved forever in everything, and that cause and effect are exactly equivalent even to the slightest circumstance, although each effect depends upon an infinity of causes and every cause has an infinity of effects. It would not be possible to obtain this state of things, if the essence of the body consisted only in a certain form, motion or modification of extension, which was predetermined. Furthermore, there is nothing of the kind in nature; taken strictly, every thing is indefinite with regard to extension, and whatever we attribute to bodies are only phenomena and abstractions: this enables us to see how easy it is to fall into error if reflections so necessary for recognizing the true principles and for having a valid idea of the universe are not made. It seems to me that as much prejudice is displayed in refusing to accept so reasonable an idea as this, as there would be in not recognizing the grandeur of the world, the subdivision to infinity and the mechanical explanations of nature. It is as great an error to conceive of extension as a primitive concept without looking into the real concept of substance and of action, as it was formerly to be contented with considering substantial forms as a whole without entering into details as to the modifications of extension.

The great number of souls (to which, however, I do not necessarily attribute in every case pain and pleasure), should not trouble us any more than do the great number of the atoms put forward by Gassendi, which are quite as indestructible as the soul. On the contrary it is one of the perfections of nature to have so many of them, since a soul or indeed a living substance is infinitely more perfect than an atom, which is without variety or subdivision. Every living thing contains a world of diversity in a real unity. Our experience is in favor of this great number of living things; we find that there is a prodigious quantity of them in a drop of water tinctured with powder and with one blow millions of them can be killed so that neither the frogs of the Egyptians nor the quails of the Israelites of which you spoke, M., at all approach the number. Now, if these animals have souls, the same must be said of their souls which can probably be said of the animals themselves; namely, that they have been

living from the very creation of the world and that
they will live to its end, and that birth being apparently only a change consisting in growth, so death
is only a change or diminution which causes this
animal to re-enter into the engulfing of a world of
minute creatures, where perceptions are very limited until the command comes calling them to return
to the theater of action. The ancients made the
mistake of introducing the transmigration of souls,
in place of the transformation of the same animal
which always preserves the same soul. They put
metempsychoses in place of metaschematismi.
Spirits, however, are not subjected to these revolutions, or' rather these revolutions of bodies must
serve the divine economy for the sake of spirits.
God creates them when it is time and he detaches
them from the body, at least from the material
body by death; since they must always preserve
their moral qualities and their memory in order to
be perpetual citizens of that universal republic,
absolutely perfect, whose monarch is God. This
republic can never lose any of its members and its
laws are superior to those of the body. I grant that
bodies by themselves without the soul have only a
unity of aggregation, but the reality which inheres
in them comes from the parts which compose them
and which retain their substantial unity through the
living bodies that are included in them without number.

Nevertheless, although it is possible that a soul
have a body made up of animated parts or of separate souls, the soul or the form of the whole is not,
therefore, composed of souls or forms of parts. In
regard to an insect which is cut in two, it is not

necessary that the two parts shall remain animated, although there may be some movement in them, at least the soul of the whole insect will remain only on one side and as in the formation and in the growth of the insect the soul has already been in a certain part alive from the very start, it will remain also after the destruction of the insect, still alive in a certain part, which will always be as small as is necessary to serve as an asylum from the action of him who is tearing or destroying the body of this insect. We need not, however, imagine with the Jews that there is a little bone of irrefrangible hardness where the soul preserves itself.

I agree that there are degrees of accidental unity, that a regulated society has more unity than a confused mob and that an organized body or indeed a machine has more unity than a society. That is, it is more appropriate to conceive of them as a single thing because there is more relation between the component elements. All these unities, however, receive their name only through thoughts and through appearances like colors and other phenomena that are, nevertheless, called real. The fact that a pile of stones or a block of marble can be touched does not prove its substantial reality any more successfully than the visibility of a rainbow proves its reality; and as nothing is so solid that it has not a certain degree of fluidity, perhaps the block of marble itself is only a mass of an infinite number of living bodies like a lake full of fish, although such animals in a body can be ordinarily distinguished by the eye only when the body is partially decayed. We may say of these compounds and of similar things what Democritus said very well of them, namely *esse opinione, lege, νόμῳ*. Plato had the same opinion in regard to all that is purely material. Our mind sees or conceives of certain true substances which have certain modes. These modes involve relations to other substances whenever the mind finds occasion to join them in thought and to make one name stand for the whole assembly of these things, which name shall serve as a means of reasoning; but we must not make the mistake of thinking that they are substances or veritably real beings. This position can be held only by those who go no farther than appearances, or else by those who consider as realities all the abstractions of the mind and who conceive number, time, place, motion, form and sensible quality as so many beings by themselves. I, on the contrary, hold that philosophy cannot be restored in a better way nor better reduced to precision than by recognizing substances or complete beings endowed with a true unity in which different states succeed. All the rest are to be considered only as phenomena, abstractions or relations.

Nothing will ever be found fitted to constitute a true substance out of several beings by means of aggregation; for example, if the parts which fit together for a common design are more appropriate to constitute a true substance than those which are in contact, all the officials of the India Company in Holland would constitute a real substance better than would a pile of stones. But such a common design—what is it but a resemblance, or rather an arrangement of actions and passions, which our mind sees in different things? If this unity by contact should be preferred as the most reasonable hypothesis, other difficulties would be found: the parts of solid bodies are perhaps united only by the pressure of surrounding bodies and by their own pressure, and in their substance they may have no more union than a pile of sand *arena sine calce*. Why will many rings linked together to constitute a chain compose more of a true substance than if they had openings by means of which they could be separated? It is possible that the links of a chain should not touch one another and should not even be interlinked and yet, nevertheless, unless they were taken in a certain particular way they could not be separated, as in the accompanying figure.

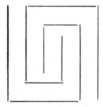

Would it be said in such a case that the substance of this compound is, as it were, in suspense, and depends upon the future cleverness of him who wishes to separate them? These are all fictions of the mind, and so far as we do not discern what is truly a complete being, or indeed, a substance, we shall have no resting place, and through this distinction of substances alone is there a means of establishing stable and real principles.

In conclusion, nothing should be considered certain without a basis. It is therefore for those who speak of beings and substances without a real unity to prove that there is more reality than that which has just been spoken of; and I am awaiting that concept of a substance or of a being which can include all those things and in accordance with which, parts and perhaps even dreams may some day pretend to reality: at least I hope that precise limits will be given to the citizenship rights which are being granted to beings formed by aggregation.

I have treated this subject at length so that you might understand not only my positions but also the reasons which have compelled me to assume them. I submit them to your judgment whose fairness and exactness I know.   I send also an article in The News of the Republic of Letters which you may find will serve as a reply to the Abbé Catelan.   I consider him an able man after what you have said, but what he has written against M. Huygens and against me, makes it clear that he goes a little too fast.   We shall see what he will do now.   I am delighted to learn of the good condition of your health ; I desire its continuation with all the zeal and all the passion which makes me, M., etc.

P. S.—I reserve for another time certain subjects which you have touched upon in your letter.

XVIII

Leibniz to Count Ernst von Hessen-Rheinfels.

April 30, 1687.

Monseigneur:

I hope that your Serene Highness will receive the book which was delayed so long; I looked for it myself at Wolfenbuttel in order that you might have it again since you were laying the blame on me. I have taken the liberty to add a letter and some

documents for M. Arnaud. I have some hope that
when he shall have read them, his penetration and
his sincerity will, perhaps, enable him to approve
entirely of that which at the beginning seemed
strange to him, because since he has modified his
position after having seen my first explanation, perhaps he will come to approbation after having seen
this last one which, in my opinion, clearly does
away with all the difficulties that he said still
troubled him. However that may be, I shall be
content if he decides, at least, that these opinions,
even though they may be very false, entail nothing
directly contrary to the definitions of the Church
and that consequently they are tolerable even in a
Roman Catholic. For your Serene Highness
knows, better than I can tell, that there are tolerable errors, and that there are even errors whose
consequences are believed to destroy the articles of
faith, and yet, nevertheless, neither these errors
nor those who hold them are condemned because
the consequences are not approved of. For example, the Thomists hold that the hypothesis of the
Molinists destroys the perfection of God; while, on
the other hand, the Molinists think that the predeter-
mination of the former destroys the freedom of
man; nevertheless, since the Church has not yet
come to any conclusion upon the matter, neither the
former nor the latter can be considered as heretics
nor their opinions as heresies. I think the same
can be said of my proposition, and for many reasons
I should like to know if M. Arnaud does not himself now acknowledge their harmlessness. He is
very busy and his time is too valuable for me to
pretend that he should employ it in discussing a

matter regarding the truth or falsehood of an opinion; but it is easy for him to decide upon its tolerability, since it is merely a question of knowing whether they are contrary to certain definitions of the Church.

XIX

Leibniz to Arnauld.

August 1st, 1687.

I have learned with much pleasure that his Serene Highness, Count Ernst, has seen and found you in good health. I hope with all my heart that I shall have such news frequently, and that the body will feel as little the effects of age as has the mind, whose energy still manifests itself. I have myself appreciated this energy, and I confess that I know no one from whom I look for a judgment upon my meditations more stable, more penetrating, and also more sincere than from you.

I do not wish to trouble you, but the material of the later letters being of an importance second only to that of religion and having great affinities with it, I confess that I should like to be able to enjoy once more your enlightenment and at least to learn your opinion in regard to my last explanations; for if you find in them an appearance of reason, I shall be confirmed, but if you find anything to say against them I shall advance more cautiously and shall be obliged to examine some day the whole subject anew.

In place of M. Catelan it was the Rev. Father Malebranche who replied a short time ago in The News of the Republic of Letters to the objection which I had put forward. He seems to realize that certain of the laws of nature or principles of motion which he advanced would be difficult to maintain ; but he thought this was because he had based them on the assumption of absolute hardness which is not found in nature, while I think that if absolute hardness could be found in nature these laws would still be untenable. It is a defect in the reasoning of Descartes and his followers not to have considered that everything that is said of motion, of inequality, and of elasticity, should also be true if things are supposed to be infinitely small. In this case motion (infinitely small) becomes rest, inequality (infinitely small) becomes equality, and elasticity (infinitely prompt) is nothing else than extreme hardness; somewhat as everything which geometers demonstrate regarding an ellipse proves true of a parabola, when conceived as an ellipse with its second focus infinitely distant. It is a remarkable thing to see that almost all Descartes' laws of motion conflict with this principle, which I hold to be quite as infallible in physics as it is in geometry, because the author of things acts as a perfect geometer. If I make any reply to Father Malebranche it will be principally in order to point out the above mentioned principle, which is of great utility and which has not as yet been generally considered, so far as I know.

But I am detaining you too long and this matter is not worthy of your attention, I am, etc.,

XX

Arnauld to Leibniz.

August 28th, 1687.

I must begin by making excuses for replying so late to your letter of April 3d. Since then I have had various illnesses and various occupations and beside it is a little hard for me to apply myself to such abstract things; I therefore ask for your consideration if I give rather briefly my opinion about the new points in your last letter.

1. I have no clear idea what you mean by the word *express* when you say that "our soul expresses more distinctly, other things being equal, that which pertains to its own body, since it expresses even all the universe in a certain sense." For if by this *expression* you mean a certain thought or a certain knowledge, I cannot agree that my soul has more thought and knowledge regarding the movement of the lymph in the lymphatic ducts than regarding the movement of the satellites of Saturn; if what you call expression is neither thought nor knowledge, I do not know what it is. Therefore it cannot be of service in solving the difficulty which I raised; namely, how my soul can have a feeling of pain when I am pricked during my sleep; since for this it would have to know that some one were pricking me, while in fact it obtains this knowledge only by the pain which it feels.

2. In regard to the following reasoning in the philosophy of occasional causes: "my hand moves as soon as I wish it; now it is not my soul which is the real cause of this motion, neither is it the body, therefore it is God"; you say that this supposes that

a body cannot move itself. Your thought, however, is that it can, and you hold that whatever there is of reality, in the state which is called motion, proceeds quite as much from the corporeal substance itself, as the thought and the will proceeds from the mind.

This is what seems to me very hard to understand, that a body which has no motion can give itself motion. And if this is admitted, one of the proofs for the being of God is destroyed; namely, the necessity for a first mover.

Moreover, if a body could give motion to itself, it would not result in my hand's moving itself every time that I wished it; for, being without knowledge, how would it know when I wished it to move itself.

3. I have more to say in regard to the indivisible and indestructible substantial forms which you think should be admitted in the case of all animals and perhaps even in the case of plants, because otherwise matter (which you consider as neither composed of atoms nor of mathematical points, but to be divisible to infinity) would not be a *unum per se* but only an *aggregatum per accidens*.

(1). I replied to you that perhaps it is an essential of matter, which is the most imperfect of all beings, not to have any true and proper unity, just as St. Augustine thought, that is, to be *plura entia* and not properly *unum ens*; and that this is no more incomprehensible than is the infinite divisibility of matter, which you admit.

But you replied that this cannot be so, because there can be no *plura entia* where there is no *unum ens*.

But how can you employ this argument, which M. Cordemoy perhaps might have thought true, but which, according to you, must be necessarily false, since, excepting animated beings, which do not form one hundred thousand thousandth part, all the rest must, in your opinion, be without substantial forms, merely *plura entia* and not properly *unum ens?* It is, therefore, not impossible that there should be *plura entia* even where there is properly no *unum ens.*

(2). I do not see that your substantial forms can remedy this difficulty, for the attribute of the *ens* which is called *unum*, taken as you take it, strictly metaphysically, must be essential and intrinsic to what is called the *unum ens.* Therefore, if a particle of matter is not a *unum ens* but *plura entia*, I do not see how a substantial form, which being really distinguished from it, could only give it an extrinsic property—how this substantial form could make it cease being a *plura entia* and should make it a *unum ens* by an intrinsic property. I understand easily that this would give us a reason for calling it *unum ens*, if we did not take the word *unum* in this metaphysical strictness. Substantial forms, however, are not called for in order to be able to give the name *one* to an infinity of inanimate bodies, because, is it not correct usage to say that the sun is one, that the earth which we inhabit is one, etc? It is not evident, therefore, that there is any necessity for admitting these substantial forms in order to give to bodies a true unity, which they would not otherwise have.

(3). You admit these substantial forms only in animate bodies.* Now there are no animate bodies

---

* Leibniz's note: "I do not remember having said that."

which are not organized, nor are there any organized bodies which are not *plura entia;* therefore your substantial forms, far from preventing bodies to which they are joined from being *plura entia,* must themselves become *plura entia* in order that they may be joined.

(4). I have no clear idea of these substantial forms or souls as applied to brutes. It must be that you regard them as substances, since you call them substantial, and since you say that only substances are truly real beings, among which you include above all these substantial forms. Now I know only two sorts of substances, bodies and minds, and it is for those who claim that there are others to show me them, according to the maxim with which you conclude your letter, *"that nothing should be considered certain without a basis."* Suppose therefore that these substantial forms are either bodily or mental; if they are bodily they must be extended and consequently divisible and divisible to infinity; hence it follows that they are not a *unum ens* but *plura entia;* just as are the physical bodies which they animate; they are not therefore able to impart a true unity. If, however, the subtantial forms are mental, their essence will be to think, for this is what I understand by the word mind. It is hard for me to understand how an oyster thinks or a worm thinks; and since you say in your last letter that you are not sure but that plants have a soul, have a life or a substantial form, it must be you are not sure that plants do not think, because their substantial forms, if they have any, not being corporeal because they are not extended, must be mental, that is to say, a substance which thinks.

(5). The indestructibility of these substantial forms or souls in brutes appears to me still more untenable. I asked you what became of the souls of these brutes when they died or when they were killed, just as when worms were burned what became of their souls. You reply "that they remain for each worm in a small part of the body that remains alive. This will always be as small as is necessary to serve as a shelter from the action of the fire which tears to pieces or which destroys the bodies of these worms." This brings you to say that "the ancients were mistaken in introducing the transmigration of souls in place of the transformation of the same animal which always preserves the same soul." Nothing can be imagined more subtle for meeting the difficulty that I raised, but you will have to be on your guard, M., against what I am about to say; when a silk moth casts its eggs each one of these eggs in your opinion has the soul of a silk worm, whence it happens that five or six months later little silk worms hatch out. Now, if a hundred of these silk worms had been burned there would be, in your opinion, a hundred souls of silk worms in so many little particles of the ashes; but on the one hand I do not know any one whom you can persuade that each silk worm after having been burned remains the same animal preserving the same soul joined now to a speck of ashes which was formerly a little portion of its own body; and, on the other hand, if this were so, why is no silk worm born out of these specks of ashes as they are born out of the eggs?

(6). This difficulty appears greater in the case of animals, where it is known certainly that they cannot be born except through the alliance of two

sexes; I ask, for example, what became of the soul
of the ram which Abraham offered in place of Isaac
and which he burned? You will not say that it passed
into the foetus of another ram, for this would be the
metempsychosis which you condemn; but you reply
that it remained in a particle of the body of this ram
reduced to ashes and that therefore it is only the
transformation of the same animal which has always
preserved the same soul. This could be said with
some appearance of truth in your hypothesis of the
substantial forms of a caterpillar which becomes a
butterfly, because the butterfly is an organized body
quite as much as is the caterpillar, and therefore it
is an animal which can be considered the same as
the caterpillar because it preserves many of the
parts of the caterpillar without any change, and the
other parts have changed only the forms. But this
part of the ram, reduced to ashes, in which the soul
of the ram has taken refuge, not being organized,
cannot be taken for an animal, and therefore the
soul of the ram which is joined to it, does not compose an animal, much less a ram, such as the soul of
a ram should. What will then become of the soul of
this ram in this cinder? For it cannot separate
itself away, to go elsewhere, since this would be a
transmigration of the soul, that you have condemned. The same is the case with an infinity of
other souls which would never form animals because
of being joined to particles of matter not organized, but which invisible could become organized
according to laws established in nature. What an
infinity of monstrous things would be this infinity
of souls joined to bodies which cannot become animated!

Not long since I saw what Abbé Catelan replied to your answer in The News of the Republic of Letters for the month of June. What he said there seemed very clear to me, perhaps however, he did not entirely understand your thought; therefore, I am awaiting the reply which you will make to him. I am, Monsieur,

Your very humble and very obedient servant,

A. A.

XXI

A. Arnauld to Count Ernst von Hessen-Rheinfels.

August 31st, 1687.

Here, M., is the reply to the last letter which M. Leibniz sent through your Serene Highness in April last. I was not able to apply myself to it sooner in order to reply to it. I beg you to send it on to him because I do not know his traits. If you will look it through you will see that there are a good many very strange opinions in regard to physics and some which appear to be hardly tenable, but I have tried to tell him my opinion regarding them in a way which should not wound him; it would be better were he to quit, for a time at least, these kinds of speculations, in order to apply himself to the most important business that he can have, which is the choice of the true religion in accordance with what he wrote to your Highness a few years ago. There is cause for fear that death may overtake him before he has taken a step so important for his salvation. M. Nicole's book against Seigneur Jurieu's new ecclesiastical system has just been printed. We are expecting it from Paris in five or six days. I will send you a copy by the Cologne stage together with certain other books which you will like to see.

XXII

Count Ernst von Hessen-Rheinfels to Leibniz.

My dear M. Leibniz:

There is reason for saying what M. Arnauld has said; for even if there were thousands among the Protestants who did not know their right hand from their left, who, in comparison with the savants, would be reputed as unthinking brutes, and who adhered only materially to heresy, certainly this cannot be said of you who have so much enlightenment, and with respect to whom, if there had never been any other but myself, as much as possible has been done to make you come forth from the Schismatics and to represent to you whatever there was to be represented. To mention merely one out of a thousand points; do you believe that Christ would have so constituted his Church that what one thought white another might think black, and that he would have constituted the ecclesiastical ministry in such a contradictory fashion that we should be in debate about it with the Protestants, we thinking one thing and you thinking another? For example, we hold that your ministers are laymen and are usurpers in the ministry. I do not know what you may think of ours who are so opposed to yours on this point. O, my dear M. Leibniz, do not lose thus the time of grace and *hodie si vocem Domini audieritis, nolite obdurare corda vestra.* Christ and Belial can no more agree together than do the Catholics and Protestants, and I know nothing which promises your salvation unless you become a Catholic.

XXIII

Leibniz to Arnauld.

October 6, 1687.

As I always hold in high esteem your criticism when you have seen the point at issue, I will try this time so to write that the positions which I hold as important and almost as certain, may appear to you, if not certain, at least as entertainable; for it does not seem to me at all difficult to answer the doubts which you still have, and which, in my opinion, result only because a person, however able he may be, when he has his mind made up and is otherwise diverted, has difficulty at first in entering into a new line of thought upon an abstract subject, where neither figures nor models nor illustrations can assist him.

I have said that the soul naturally expresses the whole universe in a particular sense and according to the relation which other bodies have to its own; consequently, as it expresses most directly that which belongs to the parts of its own bodies, it ought, in virtue of the laws of relationship which are essential to it, to express in particular certain unusual changes of its own body; for instance, that which happens when it feels pain. To this you reply that you have no clear idea of what I mean by the word express; that, if I mean by it a thought, you will not agree that the soul has any more thought and cognizance of the movement of the lymph in the lymphatic ducts than of the movements of the satellites of Saturn. If I mean, however, something else, you say you do not know what it is, and, consequently (supposing that I were not able to explain it distinctly), this word would be of no service in letting us know how the soul can become aware of the feeling of pain, since it would needs be, you say, that it already knew that I was being pricked instead of obtaining this knowledge only by the pain which it felt.

In reply to this I will explain this word which you think is obscure, and I will apply it to the difficulty which you have raised. One thing expresses another, in my use of the term, when there is a constant and regulated relation between what can be said of the one and of the other. It is thus that a projection in perspective expresses a structure. Expression is common to all forms, and is a class of which ordinary perception, animal feeling and intellectual knowledge are species. In ordinary perception and in feeling it is enough that what is divisible and material and what is found common to several beings should be expressed or represented in a single indivisible being, or in the substance which is endowed with a true unity. We cannot at all doubt the possibility of such a representation of several things in a single one, since our own souls furnish us examples; this representation, however, is accompanied by consciousness in a rational soul and becomes then what is called thought.

Now, such expression is found everywhere, because all substances sympathize with one another and receive some proportional change corresponding to the slightest motion which occurs in the whole universe. These changes, however, may be more or less noticeable, as other bodies have more or less relation with ours. I think that M. Descartes would have agreed with this himself, for he would doubtless grant that because of the continuity and divisibility of all matter the slightest movement would have its effect upon neighboring bodies and consequently from body to body to infinity, but in diminishing proportion. Thus, our bodies ought to be affected in some sort by the changes of all others. Now, to all the movements of our bodies certain perceptions or thoughts of our soul, more or less confused, correspond; therefore, the soul also will have some thought of all the movements of the universe, and in my opinion every other soul or substance will have some perception or expression of them. It is true that we do not distinctly perceive all the movements in our body, as for example the movement of the lymph, but to use an example which I have already employed, it is somewhat in the same way that I must have some perception of the motion of every wave upon the shore so that I may perceive what results from the whole; that is to say, that great sound which is heard near the sea. In the same way we feel also some indistinct result from all the movements which go on within us, but, being accustomed to this internal motion, we perceive it clearly and noticeably only when there is a considerable change, as at the beginning of an illness. It is to be desired that physicians should apply themselves to distinguish more exactly these kinds of confused feeling which we have within our bodies. Now, since we perceive other bodies only by the relation which they have to our own, I had reason for saying that the soul expresses better what belongs to its own body and knows the satellites of Jupiter and of Saturn only in accordance with a motion which is produced within the eye. In all this I think the Cartesians would argee with me, excepting that I suppose that there are around us other souls beside our own to which I attribute a lower expression or perception than thought. For the Cartesians deny feelings to animals and do not admit any substantial forms outside of men. This does not at all affect our question here regarding the cause of pain. We have now to ask how the soul perceives the movements of its body, since there seems to be no way of explaining by what means the action of an extended mass may be transmitted to an indivisible being. Most Cartesians confess that they can give no reason for this union; the authors of the hypothesis of occasional causes think that it is a *nodus vindice dignus, cui Deus ex machina intervenire debeat,* a knot worthy of such an extricator that God must intervene to solve it. For my part, I explain it in a natural way. From the concept of substance or of complete being in general, where the present state is always a natural consequence of the preceding state, it follows that the nature of every singular substance and consequently of every singular soul is to express the universe. From the start it was created in such a way that in virtue of the laws of its own nature it is obliged to agree with whatever takes place in bodies, and particularly in its own. There is no cause for astonishment therefore, that it is of the nature of the soul to represent to itself a pricking sensation when its body is pricked: in order to explain this matter let us put on opposite sides:

State of the body at the moment A.

State of the body at the succeeding moment B (pricking).

State of the soul at moment A.

State of the soul at the moment B (pain).

Just as the state of the body at the moment B
follows the state of the body at the moment A, in
the same way the state B of the soul is a consequence of the preceding state A of the same soul,
according to the concept of substance in general.
Now, the states of the soul are naturally and essentially expressions of the corresponding states of the
world, and particularly of the bodies which belong
to them; therefore, since the pricking constitutes
a part of the condition of the body at the moment
B, the representation or expression of the pricking,
which is the pain, will also form a part of the state
of the soul at moment B; because, as one motion follows from another motion, so one representation in
a substance, whose nature it is to be representative,
follows from another repesentation. Accordingly the
soul must needs perceive the pricking when the
laws of correspondency require it to express more
distinctly some extraordinary change in the parts of
its body. It is true that the soul does not always
distinctly perceive the causes of the pricking and of
its future pain, when they are still concealed in the
representation of the state A, as when one is asleep
or for some other reason does not see the pin
approaching. This is, however, because, at such a
time, the motion of the pin makes too little impression and although we are already affected in some
sort by all the motions and representations in our
soul, and though we have thus in us the representation or expression of the causes of the pricking, and
consequently the cause of the representation of the
same pricking, that is to say, the cause of the pain,
we are yet not able to separate them out from all the
other thoughts and movements excepting when they

become quite considerable. Our soul notices only more special phenomena, which are distinguishable from others, never thinking distinctly of any one when the thought is about them all equally.

In accordance with this, I do not see that the slightest shade of difficulty can be found in this position, unless it be denied that God can create substances which are made from the start in such a way that by virtue of their own natures they agree in the series of events with the phenomena of all the others. Now, there are no plausible grounds for denying this possibility. Mathematicians represent the movements of the heavens by means of machines, (as when

> *Jura poli rerumque fidem legesque deorum*
> *Cuncta Syracusius transtulit arte senex,*

a thing which we can do much better to-day than Archimedes could in his time), and why cannot God, who infinitely surpasses these mathematicians, create from the very start representative substances in such a way that they shall express by their own laws, in accordance with the natural changes of their thoughts or representations, whatever is to happen to all bodies. This appears to me not only easy to conceive, but also worthy of God and of the beauty of the universe, and in a way a necessary conception, since all substances must have a harmony and union among themselves, and all must express in themselves the same universe and the universal cause, which is the will of their Creator, and the decrees or laws which He has so established that they fit together in the best possible way. Furthermore, this mutual correspondence of different substances which are not able, if we speak with metaphysical strictness, to act one upon another, and which, nevertheless, agree as though one were acting upon the other, is one of the strongest proofs for the existence of God or of a common cause which each effect must always express according to its point of view and its capacity. Otherwise the phenomena of different minds would not agree and there would be as many systems as substances; or rather, it would be a pure chance if they at times agreed. All the conceptions which we have of time and of space are based upon this agreement. But I should never finish, were I to explain exhaustively all that is connected with our subject; however, I prefer to be prolix rather than not to express myself sufficiently.

To go on to your other objections, I now think that you will see, M., what I mean, when I say that a corporeal substance gives to itself its own motion, or, rather, whatever there is of reality in the motion at each moment, that is, the derivative force, of which it is a consequence; for, every preceding state of a substance is a consequence of its preceding state. It is true that a body which has no motion cannot give itself motion; but I hold that there are no such bodies. (Also, strictly speaking, bodies are not pushed by others when there is a contact, but it is by their own motion or by the internal spring, which again is a motion of the internal parts. Every corporeal mass, large or small, has already in it all the force that it will ever acquire, the contact with other bodies gives it only the determination, or, better, this determination takes place only at the time that the contact does). You will say that God can reduce a body to a state of perfect repose; I reply, however, that God can also reduce it to nothing, and that this body, deprived of action and of passion, need not be considered a substance; at least, it is enough if I say that when God ever reduces a certain body to perfect repose, something that can happen only by a miracle, he would require a new miracle in order to restore any motion to it.   You see that my opinion confirms rather than destroys the proof of a prime mover: a reason must always be given for the commencement of the motion and for the laws and the agreement of the motions among themselves, and this can never be done without having recourse to God.   Furthermore, my hand does not move because I wish it for it would be in vain, unless I had a miraculous faith, for me to wish the mountain to move, and in the case of my hand I should not be able to wish its moving with success unless it were exactly at that moment that the muscles of my hand made the necessary contraction for this effect; so much the more must what I suffer agree with the changes of my body.   The one always accompanies the other in virtue of the correspondence which I established above; each one, however, has its cause immediately in itself.

I come to the point regarding the forms or the souls which I consider to be indivisible and indestructible.   I am not the first one to hold this opinion.   Parmenides, of whom Plato speaks with respect, as well as Melissus, held that there was neither generation nor corruption except in appearance.   Aristotle takes the same position in Book 3, *De cælo*, chapter 2, and the author of *De diæta*, Book I., which is attributed to Hippocrates, says expressly that an animal cannot be born wholly as a new animal nor entirely destroyed. Albertus Magnus and John Bacon seem to have thought that the substantial forms were already concealed in matter from all time; Fernel has them descend from heaven, to say nothing of those who derive them from the soul of the world. These have all seen a part of the truth, but they have not developed it. Most of them believed in the transmigration and others in the traduction of souls, instead of thinking of the transmigration and transformation of an animal already formed. Others, not being able to explain the origin of the forms, have said that they begin by a true creation. Such a creation in time I admit only in the case of reasoning souls, and hold that all the forms which do not think were created at the same time that the world was. But they believe that this creation takes place all the time whenever the smallest worm is born. Philoponus, an ancient commentator upon Aristotle, in his book against Proclus, and Gabriel Biel seem to have been of this opinion. I think that St. Thomas considered the souls of beasts as indivisible. Our Cartesians go much further when they say that every soul and every true substantial form must be indestructible and ingenerable. This is why they refused souls to beasts, although M. Descartes, in a letter to M. Morus, says that he is not certain that they have no souls. Since no special objection is made to those who speak of perduring atoms, why is it found strange when the same is said of souls to which indivisibility should belong by their very nature, especially because, if we combine the position of the Cartesians regarding the substance and the soul, with the prevailing opinion regarding the souls of beasts, the indestructibility necessarily follows. It will be difficult to overcome this opinion which has been always and everywhere received and which has been broadcast, namely, that beasts have feelings. Now, if we grant that they have souls, what I hold regarding the indestructibility of the souls is not only necessary according to the Cartesians but it is important again in ethics and in religion, in order to controvert a dangerous tenet toward which several personages of intelligence are inclined and which the Italian philosophers, who are disciples of Averroes, have disseminated; namely, that when an animal dies the particular souls return to the soul of the world. This is in contradiction to my demonstration of the nature of the individual substance and cannot be conceived of distinctly, since every individual substance must always subsist apart when once it has commenced its being; that is why the truths which I advance are so important. Those who recognize that the beasts have souls should approve of them, the others at least should not find them strange.

To come, however, to your objections regarding this indestructibility:

1. I have held that we must admit in bodies something which may be truly a single being, since matter or extended mass in itself can never be more than *plura entia*, as St. Augustine, following Plato, has very truly observed. Now, I infer that there are not several beings where there is not even one which may be truly a being, and I hold that every multitude presupposes unity; to this you make various replies, but without touching the argument itself, which is unassailable; you use only arguments

ad hominem and from inconveniences which would arise, and you try to show that what I say does not solve the difficulty. First of all, you are astonished, M., how I am able to make use of this reason, which would be apparent to M. Cordemoy who constitutes everything out of atoms, but which, from my position, as you think, would be necessarily false, since, leaving aside animated bodies that do not constitute the hundred thousand thousandth part of the universe, all the others would necessarily have to be *plura entia* and the difficulty would thus come up again. From this I see, M., that I did not explain myself sufficiently to enable you to grasp my hypothesis, for, aside from the fact that I do not remember having said that there are no substantial forms excepting souls, I am far from saying that animated bodies constitute only a small proportion of the bodies in the world; for, I think rather that everything is full of animated bodies, and in my opinion there are incomparably more souls than M. Cordemoy has atoms. His atoms are finite in number, while I hold that the number of souls, or at least of forms, is wholly infinite, and that matter being divisible without end, no portion can be obtained so small that there are not in it animated bodies, or at least such as are endowed with a primitive entelechy, and (if you will permit me to use the word life so generally), with the *vital principle*, that is to say, with corporeal substances, of all of which it may be said in general that they are alive.

2. As regards this other difficulty which you made, M., namely that the soul joined to matter does not make the latter truly one, since the matter is not really one in itself, and since the soul, as you think,

gives it only an extrinsic character I reply that it is the animated substance to which this matter belongs that is really a being, and the matter which is understood as the mass in itself is only a pure phenomenon or appearance, as well-founded, however, as is space and time. It has not even those precise and determined qualities which can enable it to pass as a determined being, as I have already indicated in what precedes, because figure itself, which is the essence of a limited extended mass, is never, strictly speaking, perfectly determined in the state of nature because of the actually infinite division of the parts of matter: there is never a globe without inequalities, never a straight line without an intermingling of curves, never a curve of a certain finite nature without an intermixture of some other, and this is as true in small portions as in large, so that far from the figure being a constitutive element in the body, it is not a quality at all real and determined outside of the thought. Never can an exact surface be assigned to any body as could be done if there were atoms; I can say the same thing of size and of motion, namely, that these qualities or predicates are phenomena like colors and sounds, and although they involve a more distinct knowledge they cannot hold up under a final analysis. Consequently extended mass, when considered without entelechies, that is, as consisting only in those qualities of size and motion, is not a corporeal substance but a wholly pure phenomenon like the rainbow. It has been also recognized by philosophers that it is the substantial form which gives a definite being to matter, and those who do not pay attention to that point will never get out of the labyrinth of the composition of the continuum if they once enter: only indivisible substances and their different states are absolutely real. This Parminedes and Plato and many other ancients have indeed seen.

However, I grant that the word *one* can be applied to a gathering together of inanimate bodies although no substantial form unites them, just as I am able to say there is one rainbow, there is one herd. But this is a unity, phenomenal or of thought, which is not sufficient for the reality back of the phenomenon. [If we take as the matter of the corporeal substance, not its formless mass but a secondary matter which is the manifold of substances whose mass constitutes the whole body, it can be said that these substances are parts of this matter; just as those which enter into our body make a part of it. It is the same with other corporeal substances as it is with our body, which is the matter and the soul, which is the form of our substance; and I find no more difficulty in this respect than is found in the case of man, in regard to whom all are agreed upon this point. The difficulties which come up in these subjects are due, among other reasons, to the fact that we have not ordinarily a sufficiently distinct conception of the whole and of the parts, because essentially the part is nothing else than an immediate requisite for the whole and is, in a way, homogeneous with it; therefore, the parts can constitute a whole, whether there is a real unity or not. It is true that the whole, which has a real unity, may continue as the same individual in the strictest sense even when it loses or gains parts as our experience shows us. In these cases the parts are immediate requisites only *pro tempore* but if, however, we understand by the term *matter* something which will always be essential to the same substance we might, in the sense of certain of the Schoolmen, understand by this the primitive passive power of a substance and, in this sense, the matter would be neither extended nor divisible although it would be the principle of divisibility or of that which stands for divisibility in the substance. However, I do not wish to argue regarding the use of terms.]

3. You object that I admit substantial forms only in the case of animated bodies—a position which I do not, however, remember to have taken. Now, you continue: all organized bodies being *plura entia* the forms or souls by no means suffice to constitute a being, but rather there must be several beings so that the body can be animated. I reply that supposing there is a soul or entelechy in beasts or in other corporeal substances, we must reason in regard to them as we all reason regarding man, who is a being endowed with a real unity; his soul gives him this unity although the mass of his body is divided into organs, ducts, humors, spirits, and that the parts are doubtless full of an infinity of other corporeal substances endowed with their own entelechies. As this third objection agrees in substance with the preceding the former solution will suffice.

4. You think that it is without a basis, when souls are attributed to animals, and you think that if they had souls there would be a mind, that is to say, a substance which thinks since we know only bodies and spirits and have no idea of any other substance; now, that an oyster thinks or a worm thinks,

it is difficult to believe. This objection applies equally to all those who are not Cartesians. Besides the fact, however, that that cannot be entirely unreasonable, which the whole human race has always accepted, namely that animals have feelings, I think I have shown that every substance is indivisible, and that consequently every corporeal substance must have a soul or at least an entelechy which has an analogy with the soul, because otherwise the body would be only a phenomenon.

To hold that every substance which is not divisible (that is to say, in my opinion, every substance in general), is a mind and must think, appears to me incomparably more rash and more destitute of basis than the conservation of forms. We know only five senses and a certain number of metals, should we conclude that there are none other in the world? It seems more evident that nature, which loves variety, has produced other forms than those which think. If I am able to prove that there are no other figures of the second degree than those found in conic sections it is because I have a distinct idea of those lines, which enables me to reach an exact division; as, however, we have no distinct idea of thought and are not able to demonstrate that the concept of an indivisible substance coincides with that of a substance which thinks, we have no cause for being certain about it. I agree that the idea which we have of thought is clear but everything which is clear is not distinct. As Father Malebranche has already noticed, it is only by internal feeling that we recognize thought, we can recognize by feeling only the things which we have experienced, and as we have not experienced the functions of other forms we must not be astonished if we have no clear idea of them; for, we ought not to have such ideas even if it were granted that there are these forms. It is a mistake to try to employ confused ideas, however clear they may be, to prove that something cannot be; and when I pay attention to distinct ideas it seems that we can conceive that phenomena which vary or which come from several beings, can be expressed or represented in a single indivisible being, and this is sufficient to constitute a perception without any necessity of adding thought or reflection to this representation. I would wish to be able to explain the differences or the degrees of the other immaterial expressions which are without thought, so that we might distinguish corporeal or living substances from animals, as far as they can be distinguished. I have not, however, meditated enough about the above, nor sufficiently examined the things in nature in order to pass judgment upon the forms as compared with their organs and activities. M. Malpighi, well versed in important analogies of anatomy, is very much inclined to think that plants can be embraced under the same class with animals and that they are imperfect animals.

5. There remains for me only to satisfy the difficulties which you have raised, M., against the indestructibility of the substantial forms; and, first of all, I am surprised that you find this point strange and untenable, because, according to your own position, all those who assign to animals a soul and feeling ought to maintain this indestructibility. These supposed difficulties are only prejudices of the mind,

which may detain common thinkers but which have no influence upon minds capable of meditation. I think it will be easy to satisfy you in regard to them. Those who perceive that there is an infinity of small animals in the least drop of water, as the experiments of M. Leewenhoeck have shown, and who do not find it strange that matter should be entirely filled with animated substances, will not find it strange either that there should be something animated in the ashes themselves, and that fire can transform an animal and reduce it, without, however, entirely destroying it. That which can be said of one caterpillar or silk-worm could be said of one hundred or one thousand, but it does not follow that we should see the silk worm re-born from the ashes. Perhaps such is not the order of nature. I know that many assure us that the generative powers remain in ashes in such a way that plants can be produced from them but I do not wish to employ doubtful experiments. Whether these small organized bodies produced by a kind of contraction from larger bodies that have become destroyed, are, as it seems wholly out of the series of generation, or whether they can come back again to the theater of action in due time, is something which I am unable to determine. These are secrets of nature where men must acknowledge their ignorance.

6. It is only apparently and as a result of the imagination that the difficulty seems greater with regard to the larger animals which are born only by the union of two sexes. This is apparently not less necessary with the smallest insects. I have recently learned that M. Leewenhoeck holds opinions quite like mine, in that he maintains that the largest ani-

mals are born by a kind of transformation. I do not dare either to approve or to reject the details of his opinion, but I hold it as true in general, and M. Swammerdam, another great investigator and anatomist, says that he also has leanings toward that opinion. Now, the opinions of these men are far more important in such matters than those of many others. True it is, I do not see that they have carried out their opinions so far as to say that corruption, and death itself, is also a transformation with respect to the living beings which are destitute of a reasonable soul, as I hold; but I think that if they were informed of my position they would not find it absurd, for there is nothing so natural as to think that that which does not begin does not perish either, and when it is acknowledged that all births are only growths or developments of an animal already formed, it is easy to be persuaded that decay or death is nothing else than the diminution or the decrease of an animal, which, nevertheless, continnes to exist and to be living and organized. It is true that it is not as easy to render this position acceptable through special experiments as it is with respect to generation, but the reason for this is evident; it is because generation advances from physical matter, little by little, so that we have time to see it, but death goes backward too much by a spring and at once returns to particles too small for us, because death occurs usually in too violent a manner for us to be able to follow out the details of this retrogression. Sleep, however, which is an image of death, and ecstacies, and the condition of the silk worm in its cocoon, which might pass for a death, also the resuscitation of flies quite drowned, through the means of a certain dry powder that may be sprinkled upon them (these flies remaining wholly dead if they are left without any assistance), and, furthermore, the state of swallows, which hibernate in the reeds, where they are found apparently dead, and the experiences of men who die from cold, from drowning or from strangulation, whom it is possible to bring to life again (in regard to which not long since a careful thinker in Germany wrote a treatise where, after having given instances known to himself personally, he exhorts those who have to do with such persons, to make more efforts than are usually made to revive them, and he describes the proper method)—all these things serve to confirm my position that these different states differ only in degree, and if we have not the means of bringing about the resuscitation after other kinds of death, it is because we do not know what must be done, or, even if we should know what must be done, our hands and our instruments and our remedies would not be successful, above all, when the dissolution goes at once into too minute particles. We must not, therefore, hold to the notions which common people may have regarding death or life, when there are both analogies and, what is better, weighty arguments to prove the contrary, for, I think, I have sufficiently shown that there must be entelechies if there are corporeal substances, and if these entelechies or souls are acknowledged, their ingenerability and indestructibility must be recognized. After this, it is incomparably more reasonable to think of the transformation of animated bodies than to conceive of the passage of souls from one body to another, which latter opinion, though very ancient, seems to be merely a form of transformation not well understood. To say that the souls of animals remain without a body or that they remain concealed in a body which is not organized, appears less natural than my position. Whether the animal resulting from the diminution of the body of the ram which Abraham sacrificed in place of Isaac should be called a ram is only a question of names, very much as would be the question whether a moth should be called a silk worm; the difficulty which you have found, M., in regard to the ram reduced to ashes comes only because I did not sufficiently explain myself. You suppose that no organized body remains in the ashes and therefore you have a right to say that it would be a monstrous thing, this infinity of souls without organized bodies; while my position is that in the state of nature there are no souls without animated bodies and no animated bodies without organs   Neither ashes nor any other mass appears to me incapable of containing organized bodies.

With regard to spirits, that is to say, substances which think and which are able to recognize God and to discover eternal truths, I hold that God governs them according to laws different from those with which he governs the rest of substances; for, while all the forms of substances express the whole universe, it can be said that animal substances express the world rather than God, while spirits express God rather than the world. God governs animal substances according to the material laws of force and of the transfer of motion, but spirits, according to spiritual laws of justice, of which the others are incapable. It is for this reason that ani-

mal substances can be called material, because the
economy which God observes with regard to them
is that of a worker or of a machinist, but with regard
to spirits God performs the functions of a Prince or
of a Legislator, which is infinitely higher;   with
regard to material substances, God is only what he
is with regard to everything, namely, the universal
author of beings.   He assumes, however, another
aspect with regard to spirits who conceive of him as
endowed with will and with moral qualities;
because he is, himself, a spirit and, like one among
us, to the point of entering with us into a social
relation, where he is the head.   It is this universal
society or republic of spirits under this sovereign
monarch which is the noblest part of the universe,
composed of so many little gods under this one
great God; for, it can be said that created spirits
differ from God only in degree, only as the finite
differs from the infinite, and it can be truly said that
the whole universe has been made only to contribute to the beautifying and to the happiness of
this city of God.   This is why everything is so constructed that the laws of force or the purely material
laws work together in the whole universe to carry
out the laws of justice or of love, so that nothing
will be able to injure the souls that are in the hands
of God, and so that everything should result for
the greatest good of those who love him; this is
why, furthermore, it must be that spirits keep their
personalities and their moral qualities so that the
city of God shall lose no member and they must in
particular preserve some sort of memory or consciousness or the power to know what they are, upon
which depends all their morality, penalties and

chastisements. Consequently, they must be exempt from those transformations of the universe which would render them unrecognizable to themselves and, morally speaking, would make another person of them. For animal substances, however, it is enough if they remain as the same individual in the metaphysical sense, while they are subjected to all imaginable changes because they are without conscience or reflection.

As far as the particulars of this condition of the human soul after death are concerned and in what way it is exempted from the transformation of things, revelation alone can give us particular instruction; the jurisdiction of the reason does not extend so far. Perhaps an objection may be made to my position when I say that God has given souls to all natural machines which are capable of them, because the souls do not interfere with one another and do not occupy any position; and that it is possible to assign to them as much perfection as they are able to have, since God has made everything in the most perfect possible manner; "there is no more a vacuum of forms than of bodies." It might be said that, by the same reasoning, God should give reasoning souls or souls capable of reflection to all animated substances. But I reply that laws superior to the laws of material nature are opposed to this, that is to say, the laws of justice, because the order of the universe would not permit justice to be observed toward all, and it would have to be, therefore, that at least no injustice should be done them; that is why they have been made incapable of reflection or consciousness, and consequently, not susceptible of happiness and unhappiness.

Finally, to recapitulate my position in a few words, I maintain that every substance involves in its present state all its past and future states and even expresses the whole universe according to its point of view, since nothing is so far from anything else that there is no relation between them. This expression would be particularly complete, however, with regard to the relations to the parts of its own body, which it expresses more immediately. Consequently, nothing happens to the substance except out of its own being and in virtue of its own laws, provided that we add the concurrence of God. It perceives other things because it expresses them naturally, having from the start been created in such a way that it can do this in a series of events, accommodating itself as called for, and it is in this agreement imposed from the beginning that consists what is called the action of one substance upon another. With regard to corporeal substances, I hold that mass, when we mean by this what is divisible, is a pure phenomenon; that every substance has a true unity in the strictness of metaphysics; that it is indivisible, ingenerable, and incorruptible; that all matter must be full of animated or, at least, living substances; that generation and corruption are only transformations from the little to the great, and *vice versa;* that there is no particle of matter in which is not found a world with an infinity of creatures organized as well as brought together; and, above all, that the works of God are infinitely greater, more beautiful, and better ordered than is commonly thought, and that mechanism, or organization, that is to say, order, is essential to them even in their smallest parts. Therefore, no hypothesis can enable

us better to recognize the wisdom of God than mine:
according to which there are everywhere substances
indicating God's perfection, and there are just so
many differing reflections of the beauty of the universe, where nothing remains empty, sterile, uncultivated and without perception. It must also be held as
indubitable that the laws of motion and the changes
of bodies serve the laws of justice and of control,
which are without doubt observed the best way possible in the government of spirits; that is to say, of
the intelligent souls which enter into social relations
with God and, together with him, constitute a kind
of perfect city of which he is the monarch.

I think now, M., that I have omitted none of all
the difficulties which you spoke of, or at least indicated, and also of those which I have thought you
might still have. It is true that this has increased
the size of this letter but it would have been more
difficult to put my meaning in less words, and had
I attempted it, obscurity might have been involved.
I think that you will now find my positions as well
articulated among themselves as with the accepted
opinions. I do not at all overthrow established
opinions, but I explain them and I carry them out
further. If you might have the leisure some day to
look over again what we finally established regarding the concept of an individual substance, you will
perhaps find, that in granting me this premise it
will be necessary to grant all the rest. I have
attempted, however, to write this letter in such a
way that it shall explain and defend itself. It is
quite possible, indeed, to separate the questions.
Those who are unwilling to recognize souls in animals and substantial forms elsewhere, may, neverthe-

less, approve of the way in which I have explained the union of the mind and the body, and all that I have said regarding true substance. It will be for them to save as they can, without such forms and without a true unity, whether by points or by atoms, as seems best to them, the reality of matter and of corporeal substances, or else to leave this undecided; since investigation can be cut off wherever one thinks best. We must not, however, stop half way when we desire to have true ideas of the universe and of the perfection of God's works, which are able to furnish us most weighty arguments with respect to God and with respect to our souls.

It is very remarkable how Catelan has so entirely missed my meaning, as you suspected he had; he advances three propositions and says that I find contradictions in them, while, in fact, I find none there, and employ these very propositions to prove the absurdity of the Cartesian principle. This is the result of dealing with men who take up things only superficially. If it can happen in a question of mathematics what should we not expect in metaphysics and in ethics. It is for this reason that I consider myself fortunate in having found in you a critic as exact as he is fair. I wish you long life, as well for the interests of the public as for my own.

I am, etc.

Part of a letter sent at the same time to Arnauld.

Here is the reply to your last objection, it has become a little long because I wish to explain myself explicitly and to leave none of your doubts untouched. Several times I inserted your own words which contributed toward increasing its size.

As I took all those positions a long time ago and have foreseen, if I might dare to say, most of the objections, they cost me hardly any meditation, and all I needed to do was to pour out my thoughts upon paper and to re-read them afterwards. I say this, M., so that you may not think me too deeply engrossed in such matters at the expense of other necessary business; you drew me on to go so far, when you made objections and questions which I wished to satisfy, as much in order to profit by your enlightenment as to make you recognize my wish to disguise nothing.

At the present time I am very busy with a history of the noble house of Brunswick. I have looked over several archives this summer and I am to make a journey in Southern Germany to seek certain documents; this does not prevent my desiring to learn your opinion regarding my explanations when your leisure will permit it and also regarding my reply to Catelan which I send herewith; I do this because it is short and, in my opinion, demonstrative, provided that it is read with the least attention. If Catelan does not do better than hitherto, I cannot expect any enlightenment from him on this subject. I wish you might be able to give a moment of serious attention to it, and you would, perhaps, be surprised to see that something which is so easy to overthrow has been accepted as an incontrovertible principle because it is clear that the velocities which bodies acquire in descending are as the square roots of the heights from which they have fallen: now, if we leave out of question external resistances a body can return exactly to the height from which it has descended, therefore———

Another draft of the above.

I herewith send you my reply to Catelan which will, perhaps, be inserted in The News of the Republic of Letters; we are at the beginning again, and I made a mistake in replying to his first answer. I should simply have said that he did not touch my objection, and should have indicated these points to which a reply was necessary, as I have now done— I have added in my reply a mechanical problem, which can be solved by geometry, but a good deal of skill must be used and I will see if M. Catelan will dare tackle it. It seems to me that he is not very able, and I am surprised to see that among so many Cartesians there are so few who imitate Descartes in trying to advance further.

XXIV

Leibniz to Count Ernst von Hessen-Rheinfels.

I beg your Highness to ask M Arnauld as well as yourself if there is really so great an evil in saying that everything (whether a species or whether an individual or person), has a certain perfect concept which involves all that can be truly said regarding it, and, according to this concept, God, who conceives of everything perfectly, conceives of the said thing? And to ask further if M. A. thinks in good faith that a man who holds such a position could not be accepted into the Catholic church, even when he sincerely rejects the supposed fatalistic consequence; and Your Highness may ask how that agrees with what M. A. formerly wrote, namely, that no trouble was made for a man in the Church on account of these kinds of opinions, and if it is not to repulse men by a useless and untimely strictness, to condemn so easily all kinds of opinions which have nothing to do with the faith?

Can it be denied that everything, whether genus, species or individual has a complete concept according to which God conceives of it (he who conceives of everything perfectly), a concept which involves or embraces all that can be said of the thing? And can it be denied that God is able to have such an individual conception of Adam or of Alexander that it shall embrace all the attributes, affections, accidents and, in general, all the predicates of this subject? And finally since St. Thomas could maintain that every separate intelligence differed in kind from every other, what evil will there be in saying the same of every person and in conceiving individuals as final species, provided that the species shall not be understood physically but metaphysically or mathematically; for, in physics when a thing engenders something similar to it, they are said to be of the same kind, but in metaphysics or in geometry we say that things differ in kind when they have any difference in the concept which suffices to describe them, so that two ellipses in one of which the major and minor axes are in the ratio of two to one and in the other in the ratio of three to one, differ in kind. Two ellipses which differ only in magnitude or proportionately, and where, in their description, there is no difference of ratio in the axes, have no specific difference or difference in kind, for it must be remembered that complete beings cannot differ merely because of differences in size.

XXV

Leibniz to Arnauld.

January 14, 1688.

Monsieur:

Perhaps you will have seen in The News of the Republic of Letters for the month of September what I replied to M. l'Abbé C. It is a remarkable thing to see how many people reply, not to what has been said, but to what they have imagined. This is what M. l'Abbé has done up to the present. For this reason it was necessary to break off abruptly, and bring him back to the first objection. I have only taken the opportunity of this argumentation to put forward a very curious geometrico-mechanical problem which I have just solved. It is to find what I call an isochronous curve, in which a body shall descend uniformly and approach equal distances to the horizon in equal times, notwithstanding the acceleration it undergoes. This latter I offset by continually changing the inclination. I did this in order to bring out something useful and to show M. l'Abbé that the ordinary analysis of the Cartesians is too limited for difficult problems. I succeeded partly in this, for M. Hugens* gave a solution of the problem in the News for October. I knew well enough that M. Hugens could do it, and therefore I didn't expect that he would take the trouble, or, at least, that he would publish his solution and set M. l'Abbé free: since, however, M. Hugens' solution is in part enigmatical, apparently to see if I can do it also, I have sent him the rest of it. Now we will see what M. l Abbé will

* So spelled by Leibniz.—*Ed.*

say about it. It is true that if the nature of the line which M. Hugens has published is known, the rest can be obtained by ordinary analysis, but without that the thing is difficult, for the converse of the rule of tangents, to find the line, having given the property of the tangents, to which this proposed problem reduces itself, is a problem which M. Descartes himself has confessed in one of his letters not to have mastered. For, usually, what I call transcendentals result, which have no degree; and when the problem reduces itself to curves of a certain degree, as it happens in this case, an ordinary analyst will have difficulty in recognizing it.

I wish, with all my heart, that you might have leisure to think over for half an hour my objection to the Cartesians, which M. l'Abbé tries to meet. Your enlightenment and your sincerity assure me that we should come to the point and that you would recognize in good faith what was the real discussion. The discussion is not long, and the matter is of importance, not only for mechanics, but also in the realm of metaphysics, because movement in itself separated from force is something merely relative and its subject cannot be determined; force, however, being something real and absolute, and its calculations, as I clearly show, different from that of motion, we must not be surprised if nature preserves the same quantity of force but not the same quantity of motion. It follows that there is in nature something besides extension and motion, unless all force or energy be denied to things, which would be to change them from substances into modes, as Spinoza does, who holds that God alone is a substance and that all other things are modifications of him. Spinoza is full of confused reveries and his pretended demonstrations *de Deo* have only an apparent truth. However, I hold that one created substance, in metaphysical strictness, does not act upon another, that is to say, with a real influence; furthermore, it is impossible to explain distinctly in what this influence consists unless we refer it to God, whose operation is a continual creation, and the source of this influence is the essential dependence of created things. If we wish to speak as ordinary men do, who say that one substance acts upon another, we must give some other conception to what is called action. It would take too long to develop this point and I refer to my last letter, which is prolix enough.

I do not know whether the Rev. Father Malebranche has replied to my answer given in one of the summer months of last year, where I advanced another general principle useful in mechanics as in geometry, which clearly overthrew all the laws of motion that Descartes put forward as well as those of Malebranche himself, together with what he said in The News to defend them.

Some day, if I find leisure I hope to write out my meditations upon the general characteristic or method of universal calculus, which should be of service in the other sciences as well as in mathematics. I have already made some successful attempts. I have definitions, axioms, and very remarkable theorems and problems in regard to coincidence, determination (or *de unico*), similitude, relation in general, power or cause, and substance, and everywhere I advance with symbols in a precise and strict manner as in algebra. I have made some applications of it in jurisprudence, and it can be truly said that there are no authors whose style approaches nearer that of the geometers than the style of the jurists in the Digests. But you will ask how is calculation to be applied to conjectural matters. I reply that it is in the way that Pascal, Hugens, and others, have given demonstrations of possible chances. Because the most probable and the most certain can always be determined in so far as it is possible to know anything *ex datis*.

I do not however wish to take more of your time, and perhaps I have already taken too much. I should not dare to do it so frequently, if the matters upon which I desire to have your criticisms were not important. I pray God to prolong your life a long time, so that we may always profit by your enlightenment. I am, with zeal, etc.

XXVI

Leibniz to Arnauld.

Venice, March 23, 1690.

I am now on the point of returning home after a long journey, undertaken under the orders of my Prince for the purpose of historical investigations. And I have found diplomas, certificates and indubitable proofs sufficient to establish the common origin of the noble Houses of Brunswick and Este, which Justel, du Cange and others had strong grounds for calling in question, because there were contradictions and errors on the part of the historians of Este in this respect, together with a complete confusion in dates and personages.

At present I am thinking of returning to my old

life and of taking up my former occupations again.
I wrote to you two years ago, a little before my
departure, and I take the same liberty again, for the
purpose of asking after your health and to let you
know how constantly the thought of your well-
known merits are in my mind. When I was at
Rome, I saw the denunciation of a new letter which
is attributed to you or to your friends. Since then
I have seen a letter of the Rev. Father Mabillon's to
one of my friends in which he says that the Rev.
Father Tellier's apology for the missionaries against
the practical morality of the Jesuits had given to
many persons favorable impressions of these Fathers,
but he had heard that you had replied to it, and that
it was said you had with geometrical logic completely overthrown the reasoning of this Father.
All this has led me to think that you are still in a
condition to render service to the public, and I pray
God that it may be so for a long time yet. It is
true that I have a personal interest in this, but it is a
praiseworthy interest since I am given a means of
being instructed, whether in common with all the
others, who will read your works, or in particular
when your criticisms shall instruct me, provided the
little leisure which you have may still permit me to
hope for this advantage at times.

As this journey has served in part to release my
mind from routine business, I have had the satisfaction of conversing with several able men on matters
of learning and science, and I have communicated
to some of them my own views, which you are
acquainted with, in order to profit by the doubts and
difficulties which they raised, and there were some
of these men who, not satisfied with the current

doctrines, found an unusual satisfaction in certain of my positions. This has led me to put them down in writing so that they may be communicated more easily, and some day, perhaps, I will have a few copies printed without my name, merely to circulate them among my friends in order to obtain their criticisms. I should like you to be able to examine them first and therefore I have made the following abstract:

A body is an aggregation of substances, and is not a substance, properly speaking. Consequently, in all bodies must be found indivisible substances which cannot be generated and are not corruptible, having something which corresponds to souls.

All these substances have been always and will always be united to organic bodies diversely transformable.

Each of these substances contains in its nature the law of the continuous progression of its own workings and all that has happened to it and all that will happen to it.

Excepting the dependence upon God, all these activities come from its own nature.

Each substance expresses the whole universe, some substances, however, more distinctly than others, each one especially distinctly with regard to certain things and according to its own point of view.

The union of the soul with the body and even the action of one substance upon another consists only in the perfect mutual accord, expressly established by the ordinance of the first creation, by virtue of which each substance following its own laws falls in with what the others require, and thus the activities of the one follow or accompany the activities or changes of the other.

Intellects, or souls which are capable of reflection and of knowing the eternal truths and God, have many privileges that exempt them from the transformations of bodies.

In regard to them moral laws must be added to physical laws.

It is for them principally that every thing has been made.

They, taken together, constitute the Republic of the Universe, with God as the monarch.

There is perfect justice and order observed in this city of God, and there is no evil action without its chastisement, nor any good action without its proportionate reward.

The better things are understood, the more are they found beautiful and conformable to the desires which a wise man might form.

We must always be content with the ordering of the past because it has absolutely conformed to the will of God, which can be known by the events, but we must try to make the future, in so far as it depends upon us, conform to the presumptive will of God or to his commandments, to beautify our Sparta and to labor in well-doing, without, however, being cast down when unsuccessful, in the firm belief that God will know how to find the most fitting times for changes to the better.

Those who are not content with the ordering of things cannot boast of loving God properly.

Justice is nothing else than love felt by the wise.

Charity is universal benevolence whose fulfillment

the wise carry out conformably to the dictates of reason so as to obtain the greatest good.

Wisdom is the science of happiness or of the means of attaining the lasting contentment which consists in the continual achievement of a greater perfection or at least in variations of the same degree of perfection.

In regard to the subject of physics: the nature of force must be understood as wholly different from motion, which is something more relative. Force must be measured by the quantity of effect: there is an absolute force, a directive force and a respective force.

Each of these forces is conserved in the same quantity in the universe, or in each machine which has no communication with others, and the two latter forces taken together compose the former or the absolute force. The same amount of motion, however, is not conserved, for I can show that if it were, perpetual motion would be possible, and that an effect would be greater than its cause.

Some time ago I published in the *Acts of Leipsic* an essay in the domain of physics for the purpose of finding the physical causes of the astral motions. I assume as basal that every motion of a solid in a fluid, where the motion is in a curved line or the velocity is constantly changing, is derived from the motion of the fluid itself. Whence I draw the conclusion that the heavenly bodies have deferent but fluid orbs, which we may call with Descartes and with the ancients, vortexes. I think there are neither vacuums nor atoms, for these are things far removed from the perfection of God's works, and that every motion is propagated from one body to all other bodies, although more feebly as the distances are greater. Supposing that all the great globes in the universe have something analogous to magnetism, I think that in addition to a certain tendency which causes them to maintain the parallelism of their axes, they have a kind of attraction whence arises something comparable to gravity. We can picture this by imagining rays of some material substance which is trying to move away from a center and consequently pushes others which have not this tendency toward the center. We may compare these rays of attraction with those of light, and by the same law which holds in illumination we shall find that the attraction is inversely as the square of the distance.

These things agree wonderfully with the phenomena. Kepler found that in general the areas of the orbits of the planets described by radii drawn from the sun to the orbits are in proportion to the times of the revolutions around the sun, and I have demonstrated an important general proposition, namely, that all those bodies which revolve in harmonic motion (that is to say, so move that their distances from the center are in arithmetical progression, while their velocities are in harmonic progression or inversely as the distances), and moreover, if these bodies have a paracentric motion (that is to say, are heavy or light as regards the same center, whatever law this attraction or repulsion may obey)—all such bodies describe areas which vary necessarily as the times, just as Kepler observed in the case of the planets. I conclude that the deferent fluid orbs of the planets revolve harmonically, and I give an *a priori* reason for this. Now, empirically observing that in fact this motion is elliptical, I find that the law of paracentric motions, which when combined with the harmonic revolutions describe ellipses, ought to be such that the attraction is inversely as the squares of the distances, that is, exactly the same as what we found above to be true *a priori* by the laws of radiation. From this I then deduce special characteristics and the whole was broached in my publication in the *Acts of Leipsic* some time ago.

I will say nothing of my calculus of increments or differences, by which I determine the tangents without eliminating irrationals and fractions even when unknown quantities are involved in them and by which I subject quadratics and transcendental problems to analysis. Neither will I speak of an entirely new analysis confined to Geometry and differing entirely from Algebra, and even less of certain other subjects which I have not yet had the time to develop. I should have liked to be able to explain them all to you in a few words, so as to have upon them your opinion, which would be of infinite service to me, had you as much leisure as I have deference for your criticism. Your time, however, is too precious, and my letter is already quite long. Therefore I bring it to an end here, and am sincerely, etc.

THE MONADOLOGY.

THE MONADOLOGY.

1. The Monad, of which we will speak here, is nothing else than a simple substance, which goes to make up composites; by simple, we mean without parts.

2. There must be simple substances because there are composites; for a composite is nothing else than a collection or *aggregatum* of simple substances.

3. Now, where there are no constituent parts there is possible neither extension, nor form, nor divisibility. These Monads are the true Atoms of nature, and, in fact, the Elements of things.

4. Their dissolution, therefore, is not to be feared and there is no way conceivable by which a simple substance can perish through natural means.

5. For the same reason there is no way conceivable by which a simple substance might, through natural means, come into existence, since it can not be formed by composition.

6. We may say then, that the existence of Monads can begin or end only all at once, that is to say, the Monad can begin only through creation and end only through annihilation. Composites, however, begin or end gradually

7. There is also no way of explaining how a Monad can be altered or changed in its inner being by any other created thing, since there is no possibility of transposition within it, nor can we conceive

of any internal movement which can be produced, directed, increased or diminished there within the substance, such as can take place in the case of composites where a change can occur among the parts. The Monads have no windows through which anything may come in or go out. The Attributes are not liable to detach themselves and make an excursion outside the substance, as could *sensible species* of the Schoolmen. In the same way neither substance nor attribute can enter from without into a Monad.

8. Still Monads must needs have some qualities, otherwise they would not even be existences. And if simple substances did not differ at all in their qualities, there would be no means of perceiving any change in things. Whatever is in a composite can come into it only through its simple elements and the Monads, if they were without qualities, since they do not differ at all in quantity, would be indistinguishable one from another. For instance, if we imagine *a plenum* or completely filled space, where each part receives only the equivalent of its own previous motion, one state of things would not be distinguishable from another.

9. Each Monad, indeed, must be different from every other. For there are never in nature two beings which are exactly alike, and in which it is not possible to find a difference either internal or based on an intrinsic property.

10. I assume it as admitted that every created being, and consequently the created Monad, is subject to change, and indeed that this change is continuous in each.

11. It follows from what has just been said, that

the natural changes of the Monad come from an internal principle, because an external cause can have no influence upon its inner being.

12. Now besides this principle of change there must also be in the Monad a manifoldness which changes. This manifoldness constitutes, so to speak, the specific nature and the variety of the simple substances.

13. This manifoldness must involve a multiplicity in the unity or in that which is simple. For since every natural change takes place by degrees, there must be something which changes and something which remains unchanged, and consequently there must be in the simple substance a plurality of conditions and relations, even though it has no parts.

14. The passing condition which involves and represents a multiplicity in the unity, or in the simple substance, is nothing else than what is called Perception. This should be carefully distinguished from Apperception or Consciousness, as will appear in what follows. In this matter the Cartesians have fallen into a serious error, in that they treat as non-existent those perceptions of which we are not conscious. It is this also which has led them to believe that spirits alone are Monads and that there are no souls of animals or other Entelechies, and it has led them to make the common confusion between a protracted period of unconsciousness and actual death. They have thus adopted the Scholastic error that souls can exist entirely separated from bodies, and have even confirmed ill-balanced minds in the belief that souls are mortal.

15. The action of the internal principle which brings about the change or the passing from one

perception to another may be called Appetition. It is true that the desire (*l'appetit*) is not always able to attain to the whole of the perception which it strives for, but it always attains a portion of it and reaches new perceptions.

16. We, ourselves, experience a multiplicity in a simple substance, when we find that the most trifling thought of which we are conscious involves a variety in the object. Therefore all those who acknowledge that the soul is a simple substance ought to grant this multiplicity in the Monad, and Monsieur Bayle should have found no difficulty in it, as he has done in his *Dictionary*, article "Rorarius."

17. It must be confessed, however, that Perception, and that which depends upon it, are inexplicable by mechanical causes, that is to say, by figures and motions. Supposing that there were a machine whose structure produced thought, sensation, and perception, we could conceive of it as increased in size with the same proportions until one was able to enter into its interior, as he would into a mill. Now, on going into it he would find only pieces working upon one another, but never would he find anything to explain Perception. It is accordingly in the simple substance, and not in the composite nor in a machine that the Perception is to be sought. Furthermore, there is nothing besides perceptions and their changes to be found in the simple substance. And it is in these alone that all the internal activities of the simple substance can consist.

18. All simple substances or created Monads may be called Entelechies, because they have in themselves a certain perfection (ἔχουσι τὸ ἐντελές). There

is in them a sufficiency (αὐτάρκεια) which makes them the source of their internal activities, and renders them, so to speak, incorporeal Automatons.

19. If we wish to designate as soul everything which has perceptions and desires in the general sense that I have just explained, all simple substances or created Monads could be called souls. But since feeling is something more than a mere perception I think that the general name of Monad or Entelechy should suffice for simple substances which have only perception, while we may reserve the term Soul for those whose perception is more distinct and is accompanied by memory.

20. We experience in ourselves a state where we remember nothing and where we have no distinct perception, as in periods of fainting, or when we are overcome by a profound, dreamless sleep. In such a state the soul does not sensibly differ at all from a simple Monad. As this state, however, is not permanent and the soul can recover from it, the soul is something more.

21. Nevertheless it does not follow at all that the simple substance is in such a state without perception. This is so because of the reasons given above; for it cannot perish, nor on the other hand would it exist without some affection and the affection is nothing else than its perception. When, however, there are a great number of weak perceptions where nothing stands out distinctively, we are stunned; as when one turns around and around in the same direction, a dizziness comes on, which makes him swoon and makes him able to distinguish nothing. Among animals, death can occasion this state for quite a period.

22. Every present state of a simple substance is a natural consequence of its preceding state, in such a way that its present is big with its future.

23. Therefore, since on awakening after a period of unconsciousness we become conscious of our perceptions, we must, without having been conscious of them, have had perceptions immediately before; for one perception can come in a natural way only from another perception, just as a motion can come in a natural way only from a motion.

24. It is evident from this that if we were to have nothing distinctive, or so to speak prominent, and of a higher flavor in our perceptions, we should be in a continual state of stupor. This is the condition of Monads which are wholly bare.

25. We see that nature has given to animals heightened perceptions, having provided them with organs which collect numerous rays of light or numerous waves of air and thus make them more effective in their combination. Something similar to this takes place in the case of smell, in that of taste and of touch, and perhaps in many other senses which are unknown to us. I shall have occasion very soon to explain how that which occurs in the soul represents that which goes on in the sense-organs.

26. The memory furnishes a sort of consecutiveness which imitates reason but is to be distinguished from it. We see that animals when they have the perception of something which they notice and of which they have had a similar previous perception, are led by the representation of their memory to expect that which was associated in the preceding perception, and they come to have feelings like those which they had before. For instance, if a stick be

shown to a dog, he remembers the pain which it has caused him and he whines or runs away.

27. The vividness of the picture, which comes to him or moves him, is derived either from the magnitude or from the number of the previous perceptions. For, oftentimes, a strong impression brings about, all at once, the same effect as a long-continued habit or as a great many re-iterated, moderate perceptions.

28. Men act in like manner as animals, in so far as the sequence of their perceptions is determined only by the law of memory, resembling the *empirical physicians* who practice simply, without any theory, and we are empiricists in three-fourths of our actions. For instance, when we expect that there will be day-light to-morrow, we do so empirically, because it has always happened so up to the present time. It is only the astronomer who uses his reason in making such an affirmation.

29. But the knowledge of eternal and necessary truths is that which distinguishes us from mere animals and gives us reason and the sciences, thus raising us to a knowledge of ourselves and of God. This is what is called in us the Rational Soul or the Mind.

30. It is also through the knowledge of necessary truths and through abstractions from them that we come to perform Reflective Acts, which cause us to think of what is called the I, and to decide that this or that is within us. It is thus, that in thinking upon ourselves we think of *being*, of *substance*, of the *simple* and *composite*, of a *material* thing and of *God* himself, conceiving that what is limited in us is in him without limits. These Reflective Acts furnish the principal objects of our reasonings.

31. Our reasoning is based upon two great principles: first, that of Contradiction, by means of which we decide that to be false which involves contradiction and that to be true which contradicts or is opposed to the false.

32. And second, the principle of Sufficient Reason, in virtue of which we believe that no fact can be real or existing and no statement true unless it has a sufficient reason why it should be thus and not otherwise. Most frequently, however, these reasons cannot be known by us.

33. There are also two kinds of Truths: those of Reasoning and those of Fact. The Truths of Reasoning are necessary, and their opposite is impossible. Those of Fact, however, are contingent, and their opposite is possible. When a truth is necessary, the reason can be found by analysis in resolving it into simpler ideas and into simpler truths until we reach those which are primary.

34. It is thus that with mathematicians the Speculative Theorems and the practical Canons are reduced by analysis to Definitions, Axioms, and Postulates.

35. There are finally simple ideas of which no definition can be given. There are also the Axioms and Postulates or, in a word, the primary principles which cannot be proved and, indeed, have no need of proof. These are identical propositions whose opposites involve express contradictions.

36. But there must be also a sufficient reason for contingent truths or truths of fact; that is to say, for the sequence of the things which extend throughout the universe of created beings, where

the analysis into more particular reasons can be continued into greater detail without limit because of the immense variety of the things in nature and because of the infinite division of bodies. There is an infinity of figures and of movements, present and past, which enter into the efficient cause of my present writing, and in its final cause there are an infinity of slight tendencies and dispositions of my soul, present and past.

37. And as all this detail again involves other and more detailed contingencies, each of which again has need of a similar analysis in order to find its explanation, no real advance has been made. Therefore, the sufficient or ultimate reason must needs be outside of the sequence or series of these details of contingencies, however infinite they may be.

38. It is thus that the ultimate reason for things must be a necessary substance, in which the detail of the changes shall be present merely potentially, as in the fountain-head, and this substance we call God.

39. Now, since this substance is a sufficient reason for all the above mentioned details, which are linked together throughout, *there is but one God, and this God is sufficient.*

40. We may hold that the supreme substance, which is unique, universal and necessary with nothing independent outside of it, which is further a pure sequence of possible being, must be incapable of limitation and must contain as much reality as possible.

41. Whence it follows that God is absolutely perfect, perfection being understood as the magnitude

of positive reality in the strict sense, when the limitations or the bounds of those things which have them are removed. There where there are no limits, that is to say, in God, perfection is absolutely infinite.

42. It follows also that created things derive their perfections through the influence of God, but their imperfections come from their own natures, which cannot exist without limits. It is in this latter that they are distinguished from God. An example of this original imperfection of created things is to be found in the natural inertia of bodies.

43. It is true, furthermore, that in God is found not only the source of existences, but also that of essences, in so far as they are real. In other words, he is the source of whatever there is real in the possible. This is because the Understanding of God is in the region of eternal truths or of the ideas upon which they depend, and because without him there would be nothing real in the possibilities of things, and not only would nothing be existent, nothing would be even possible.

44. For it must needs be that if there is a reality in essences or in possibilities or indeed in the eternal truths, this reality is based upon something existent and actual, and, consequently, in the existence of the necessary Being in whom essence includes existence or in whom possibility is sufficient to produce actuality.

45. Therefore God alone (or the Necessary Being) has this prerogative that if he be possible he must necessarily exist, and, as nothing is able to prevent the possibility of that which involves no bounds, no negation, and consequently, no contradiction, this

alone is sufficient to establish *a priori* his existence. We have, therefore, proved his existence through the reality of eternal truths. But a little while ago we also proved it *a posteriori*, because contingent beings exist, which can have their ultimate and sufficient reason only in the necessary being which, in turn, has the reason for existence in itself.

46. Yet we must not think that the eternal truths being dependent upon God are therefore arbitrary and depend upon his will, as Descartes seems to have held, and after him Monsieur Poiret. This is the case only with contingent truths which depend upon fitness or the choice of the greatest good; necessary truths on the other hand depend solely upon his understanding and are the inner objects of it.

47. God alone is the ultimate unity or the original simple substance, of which all created or derivative Monads are the products, and arise, so to speak, through the continual outflashings of the divinity from moment to moment, limited by the receptivity of the creature to whom limitation is an essential.

48. In God are present: Power, which is the source of everything; Knowledge, which contains the details of the ideas; and, finally, Will, which produces or effects changes in accordance with the principle of the greatest good. To these correspond in the created Monad, the subject or the basis of the faculty of perception and the faculty of appetition. In God these attributes are absolutely infinite or perfect, while in the created Monads or in the entelechies (*perfectihabies*, as Hermolaus Barbarus translates this word), they are imitations approaching him in proportion to their perfection.

49. A created thing is said to act outwardly in

so far as it has perfection, and to suffer from another in so far as it is imperfect. Thus action is attributed to the Monad in so far as it has distinct perceptions, and passion or passivity is attributed in so far as it has confused perceptions.

50. One created thing is more perfect than another when we find in the first that which gives an *a priori* reason for what occurs in the second. This is why we say that one acts upon the other.

51. In the case of simple substances, the influence which one Monad has upon another is only ideal. It can have its effect only through the mediation of God, in so far as in the Ideas of God each Monad can rightly demand that God, in regulating the others from the beginning of things, should have regarded it also. For, since one created Monad cannot have a physical influence upon the inner being of another, it is only through this primal regulation that one can have dependence upon another.

52. It is thus that among created things action and passion are reciprocal. For God, in comparing two simple substances, finds in each one reasons obliging him to adapt the other to it; and consequently that which is active in certain respects is passive from another point of view,—active in so far as that which we distinctly know in it serves to give a reason for that which occurs in another, and passive in so far as the reason for what transpires in it is found in that which is distinctly known in another.

53. Now as there are an infinity of possible universes in the Ideas of God, and but one of them can exist, there must be a sufficient reason for the

choice of God which determines him to select one rather than another.

54. And this reason is to be found only in the fitness or in the degree of perfection which these worlds possess, each possible thing having the right to claim existence in proportion to the perfection which it involves.

55. This is the cause for the existence of the greatest good; namely, that the wisdom of God permits him to know it, his goodness causes him to choose it and his power enables him to produce it.

56. Now, this interconnection, relationship, or this adaptation of all things to each particular one, and of each one to all the rest, brings it about that every simple substance has relations which express all the others and that it is consequently a perpetual living mirror of the universe.

57. And as the same city regarded from different sides appears entirely different, and is, as it were, multiplied perspectively, so, because of the infinite number of simple substances, there are a similar infinite number of universes which are, nevertheless, only the aspects of a single one, as seen from the special point of view of each Monad.

58. Through this means has been obtained the greatest possible variety, together with the greatest order that may be; that is to say, through this means has been obtained the greatest possible perfection.

59. This hypothesis, moreover, which I venture to call demonstrated, is the only one which fittingly gives proper prominence to the greatness of God. Monsieur Bayle recognized this when in his *Dictionary* (article "Rorarius"), he raised objections to it; indeed, he was inclined to believe that I attrib-

uted too much to God, and more than should be attributed. But he was unable to bring forward any reason why this universal harmony, which causes every substance to express exactly all others, through the relation which it has with them, is impossible.

60. Besides, in what has just been said, can be seen the *a priori* reasons why things cannot be otherwise than they are. It is because God, in ordering the whole, has had regard to every part and in particular to each Monad whose nature it is to represent. Therefore, nothing can limit it to represent merely a part of the things. It is nevertheless true, that this representation is, as regards the details of the whole universe, only a confused representation, and is distinct only as regards a small part of them, that is to say, as regards those things which are nearest or most in relation to each Monad. If the representation were distinct as to the details of the entire universe, each Monad would be a Deity. It is not in the object represented that the Monads are limited, but in the modifications of their knowledge of the object. In a confused way they reach out to infinity or to the whole, but are limited and differentiated in the degree of their distinct perceptions.

61. In this respect composites are like simple substances. For all space is filled up; therefore, all matter is connected; and in a plenum or filled space every movement has an effect upon bodies in proportion to their distance, so that not only is every body affected by those which are in contact with it, and responds in some way to whatever happens to them, but also by means of them the

body responds to those bodies adjoining them, and their intercommunication can be continued to any distance at will. Consequently every body responds to all that happens in the universe, so that he who saw all, could read in each one what is happening everywhere, and even what has happened and what will happen. He can discover in the present what is distant both as regards space and as regards time; σύμπνοια πάντα, as Hippocrates said. A soul can, however, read in itself only what is there represented distinctly. It cannot all at once open up all its folds, because they extend to infinity.

62. Thus although each created Monad represents the whole universe, it represents more distinctly the body which specially pertains to it, and of which it constitutes the entelechy. And as the body expresses all the universe through the interconnection of all matter in the plenum, the soul also represents the whole universe in representing this body, which belongs to it in a particular way.

63. The body belonging to a Monad, which is its entelechy or soul, constitutes together with the entelechy what may be called a *living being*, and with a soul what is called an *animal*. Now, this body of a living being or of an animal is always organic, because every Monad is a mirror of the universe according to its own fashion, and, since the universe is regulated with perfect order, there must needs be order also in the representative, that is to say, in the perceptions of the soul and consequently in the body through which the universe is represented in the soul.

64. Therefore, every organic body of a living being is a kind of divine machine, or natural autom-

aton, infinitely surpassing all artificial automatons. Because a machine constructed by man's skill is not a machine in each of its parts; for instance, the teeth of a brass wheel have parts or bits which to us are not artificial products and contain nothing in themselves to show the use to which the wheel was destined in the machine. The machines of nature, however, that is to say, living bodies, are still machines in their smallest parts *ad infinitum.* Such is the difference between nature and art, that is to say, between Divine art and ours.

65. The author of nature has been able to employ this divine and infinitely marvellous artifice, because each portion of matter is not only, as the ancients recognized, infinitely divisible, but also because it is really divided without end, every part into other parts, each one of which has its own proper motion. Otherwise it would be impossible for each portion of matter to express all the universe.

66. Whence we see that there is a world of created things, of living beings, of animals, of entelechies, of souls, in the minutest particle of matter.

67. Every portion of matter may be conceived as like a garden full of plants, and like a pond full of fish. But every branch of a plant, every member of an animal, and every drop of the fluids within it, is also such a garden or such a pond.

68. And although the ground and the air which lies between the plants of the garden, and the water which is between the fish in the pond, are not themselves plant or fish, yet they nevertheless contain these, usually so small, however, as to be imperceptible to us.

69. There is, therefore, nothing uncultivated, or

sterile or dead in the universe, no chaos, no confusion, save in appearance; somewhat as a pond would appear at a distance when we could see in it a confused movement, and so to speak, a swarming of the fish, without, however, discerning the fish themselves.

70. It is evident, then, that every living body has a dominating entelechy, which in animals is the soul. The parts, however, of this living body are full of other living beings, plants and animals, which, in turn, have each one its entelechy or dominating soul.

71. This does not mean, as some who have misunderstood my thought have imagined, that each soul has a quantity or portion of matter appropriated to it or attached to itself for ever, and that it consequently owns other inferior living beings destined to serve it always; because all bodies are in a state of perpetual flux like rivers, and the parts are continually entering in and passing out.

72. The soul, therefore, changes its body only gradually and by degrees, so that it is never deprived all at once of all its organs. There is frequently a metamorphosis in animals, but never metempsychosis or a transmigration of souls. Neither are there souls wholly separate from bodies, nor bodiless spirits. God alone is without body.

73. This is also why there is never absolute generation or perfect death in the strict sense, consisting in the separation of the soul from the body. That which we call generation is development and growth, and that which we call death is envelopment and diminution.

74. Philosophers have been much perplexed in

accounting for the origin of forms, entelechies, or souls. To-day, however, when it has been learned through careful investigations made in plant, insect, and animal life, that the organic bodies of nature are never the product of chaos or putrefaction, but always come from seeds in which there was without doubt some *preformation*, it has been decided that not only is the organic body already present before conception, but also that a soul, in a word, the animal itself, is also in this body; and it has been decided that, by means of conception the animal is disposed for a great transformation, so as to become an animal of another species. We can see cases somewhat similar outside of generation when grubs become flies and caterpillars become butterflies.

75. These little animals, some of which, by conception, become large animals, may be called spermatic. Those among them which remain in their species, that is to say, the greater part, are born, multiply, and are destroyed, like the larger animals. There are only a few chosen ones which come out upon a greater stage.

76. This, however, is only half the truth. I believe, therefore, that if the animal never actually commences in nature, no more does it by natural means come to an end. Not only is there no generation, but also there is no entire destruction or absolute death. These reasonings, carried on *a posteriori*, and drawn from experience, accord perfectly with the principles which I have above deduced *a priori*.

77. Therefore, we may say, that not only the soul (the mirror of an indestructible universe) is indestructible, but also the animal itself is, although its

mechanism is frequently destroyed in parts and although it puts off and takes on organic coatings.

78. These principles have furnished me the means of explaining on natural grounds the union, or, rather the conformity between the soul and the organic body. The soul follows its own laws, and the body has its laws. They are fitted to each other in virtue of the pre-established harmony between all substances, since they are all representations of one and the same universe.

79. Souls act in accordance with the laws of final causes through their desires, purposes and means. Bodies act in accordance with the laws of efficient causes or of motion. The two realms, that of efficient causes and that of final causes, are in harmony, each with the other.

80. Descartes saw that souls cannot at all impart force to bodies, because there is always the same quantity of force in matter. Yet, he thought that the soul could change the direction of bodies. This was, however, because at that time the law of nature, which affirms also the conservation of the same total direction in the motion of matter, was not known. If he had known that law, he would have fallen upon my system of Pre-established Harmony.

81. According to this system bodies act as if (to suppose the impossible) there were no souls at all, and souls act as if there were no bodies, and yet both body and soul act as if the one were influencing the other.

82. Although I find that essentially the same thing is true of all living things and animals, which we have just said, namely, that animals and souls

begin from the very commencement of the world and that they come to an end no more than does the world, there is, as far as minds or rational souls are concerned nevertheless, this thing peculiar, that their little spermatic progenitors, as long as they remain such, have only ordinary or sensuous souls, but those of them which are, so to speak, elevated, attain by actual conception to human nature, and their sensuous souls are raised to the rank of reason and to the prerogative of minds.

83. Among the differences that there are between ordinary souls and spirits, some of which I have already instanced, there is also this that, while souls in general are living mirrors or images of the universe of created things, minds are also images of the Deity himself or of the author of nature. They are capable of knowing the system of the universe, and to imitate it somewhat by means of architectonic patterns, each mind being like a small divinity in its sphere.

84. Therefore, spirits are able to enter into a sort of social relationship with God, and with respect to them he is not only what an inventor is to his machine (as is his relation to the other created things), but he is also what a prince is to his subjects, and even what a father is to his children.

85. Whence it is easy to conclude that the totality of all the spirits must compose the city of God, that is to say, the most perfect state that is possible under the most perfect monarch.

86. This city of God, this truly universal monarchy, is a moral world within the natural world. It is what is noblest and most divine among the works of God. And in it consists in reality the glory of

God, because he would have no glory were not his greatness and goodness known and wondered at by spirits. It is also in relation to this divine city that God properly has goodness. His wisdom and his power are shown everywhere.

87. As we established above that there is a perfect harmony between the two natural realms of efficient and final causes, it will be in place here to point out another harmony which appears between the physical realm of nature and the moral realm of grace, that is to say, between God, considered as the architect of the mechanism of the world and God considered as the Monarch of the divine city of spirits.

88. This harmony brings it about that things progress of themselves toward grace along natural lines, and that this earth, for example, must be destroyed and restored by natural means at those times when the proper government of spirits demands it, for chastisement in the one case and for a reward in the other.

89. We can say also that God, the Architect, satisfies in all respects God the Law-Giver, that therefore sins will bring their own penalty with them through the order of nature, and because of the very mechanical structure of things. And in the same way the good actions will attain their rewards in mechanical ways through their relation to bodies, although this cannot, and ought not, always to take place without delay.

90. Finally, under this perfect government, there will be no good action unrewarded and no evil action unpunished; everything should turn out for the well-being of the good; that is to say, of those

who are not disaffected in this great state, who, after having done their duty, trust in Providence and who love and imitate, as is meet, the Author of all Good, delighting in the contemplation of his perfections according to the nature of that genuine, pure love which finds pleasure in the happiness of those who are loved. It is for this reason that wise and virtuous persons work in behalf of everything which seems conformable to the presumptive or antecedent will, and are, nevertheless, content with what God actually brings to pass through his secret, consequent and determining will, recognizing that if we were able to understand sufficiently well the order of the universe, we should find that it goes beyond all the desires of the wisest of us, and that it is impossible to have it better than it is, not only for all in general, but also for each one of us in particular, provided that we cleave as we should to the Author of all. For he is not only the Architect and the efficient cause of our being, but he is also our Lord and the Final Cause, who ought to be the whole goal of our will, and who, alone, can make our happiness.